Knitting the
Perfect Fit

Essential Fully Fashioned Shaping Techniques
for Designer Results

Melissa Leapman

POTTER
CRAFT

NEW YORK

Copyright © 2012 by Melissa Leapman
Photographs copyright © 2012 by Potter Craft

All rights reserved.
Published in the United States by Potter Craft, an imprint
of the Crown Publishing Group, a division of Random
House, Inc., New York.
www.pottercraft.com
www.crownpublishing.com

POTTER CRAFT and colophon is a registered trademark
of Random House, Inc.

Library of Congress Cataloging-in-Publication Data
Leapman, Melissa.
  Knitting the perfect fit / by Melissa Leapman.—1st ed.
      p. cm.
1. Knitting. 2. Tailoring (Women's) I. Title.
  TT825.L388176 2012
  746.43'2—dc23   2011042936

ISBN 978-0-307-58664-3
eISBN 978-0-307-96572-1

Printed in China

Design by Jenny Kraemer
Photographs by Heather Weston
Technical illustrations by Joni Coniglio
Charts and schematic illustrations by Melissa Leapman
Technical editing by Charlotte Quiggle

Thanks to the Craft Yarn Council of America
(www.yarnstandards.com) for its Standard Yarn
Weight system chart, which appears on page 158.

10 9 8 7 6 5 4 3 2 1
First Edition

For MPB

Acknowledgments

Special thanks go to the following knitters for their help testing the patterns and creating the samples for this project: Mink Barrett, Diane Bloomer, Patricia Bluestein, Didi Bottini, Meg Croft, Marie Duquette, Lynn Gates, Jessy Henderson, Susan Hope, Tom Jensen, Cheryl Keeley, Robin May, Joan Murphy, Candace Musmeci, Holly Neiding, Dawn Penny, Judy Seip, and Angie Tzoumakas.

I am grateful to Cascade Yarn Company for providing all the yarn used in the Designer Workshops. With great stitch definition and a million and one colors, their Cascade 220 is a pleasure to design with!

Once again, I've been fortunate to surround myself with the best folks in the business: Thank you, Charlotte Quiggle, for all you do for the team. I've enjoyed our daily lunches immensely! And to Joni Coniglio: I am one *very* lucky author to have been able to work with you again. I'm sure my readers will gladly agree. . . .

Contents

Introduction

It's all in the details! The use of

what designers call fully fashioned shaping marks the difference between an ordinary ho-hum sweater and an undeniably spectacular fashion garment. Using mirrored increases and decreases—slanting certain stitches toward the left or the right to create design details can easily give a garment a **couture** touch. It is the construction difference between an $80 J.Crew cashmere V-neck sweater and the one that sells for $200 in the same catalog. Though both are knitted out of the same soft yarn, the less expensive sweater is usually made by assembling front, back, or sleeve pieces cut from huge bolts of machine-knit fabric and then sewn with a serger, while the more expensive sweater is created with hand-manipulated, machine-made knitting stitches.

Many handknitters already use **shaping details** in their garments: decreases for armholes, necklines, or sleeve caps and increases for sleeves. We don't cut our pieces into shape, we *knit* them into shape! But most knitters do not understand how shaping works or how to use simple increases and decreases to add **visual interest** to their garments. I've taught these techniques to hundreds of knitters, and during my workshop they begin to look at their knitting in a whole new way. I still remember that exciting aha! moment when a student in one of my classes worked her first fully fashioned V neckline a few years ago. "It's so neat and perfect," she proudly proclaimed. In these pages we will explore simple **fully fashioned techniques** and how to apply them to create interesting designer elements and flattering shaping details in garments for any body shape. You will learn that just adding a few extra details can take any project to an entirely new level of sophistication.

Chapter 1 of this book is a refresher course on all the basics any knitter will need to master, from different increase and decrease methods, to Knitting Charts 101, and the dos and don'ts of figure flattery. Chapter 2 illustrates simple ways to incorporate fully fashioned shaping in stockinette garments. Included are four wearable—and knittable!—projects to get your needles clicking as you practice these basic shaping techniques. Chapter 3 provides ways of using fully fashioned shaping for **designer details** such as decorative raglan seams and figure-flattering vertical lines. Many of the projects include incorporated neckbands and armbands to make the finishing of the garment faster and easier. Chapter 4 delves into exciting ways to use strategically placed **increases and decreases** to create figure-flattering sweaters. Some of the projects in this section even use fully fashioned details to fool the eye and create the *illusion* of shape: You don't have to have a perfect hourglass shape to look great!

Throughout the book, you'll discover little **body shape icons** ▲▼●■ X that will direct you to garments that are specifically designed for your individual figure type. Diagonal lines will draw attention to certain sections of the garment—and of your body. If you're going to take the time—and spend the money—to make custom garments, you might as well knit flattering ones!

You'll have fun experimenting with fully fashioned designer details—and using your knitting prowess to create **knockout pieces** that fit and flatter. Let's get started. . . .

1

Basics

No matter your skill level, superbly knit and figure-flattering garments can be made by anyone. If you're going to spend your free time (not to mention your precious yarn budget!) to create a sweater, the result ought to be as beautiful on you as possible. In this chapter, you'll learn the ins and outs of increases, decreases, knitting charts, and the simple abbreviations you'll encounter throughout the book.

What Makes a Garment Fully Fashioned?

Have you ever wondered why some ready-to-wear sweaters cost so much more than others, even when they are machine-knit? Less expensive garments are cut and sewn out of huge bolts of machine-knit fabric: using a template similar to a sewing pattern, the front, back, and sleeves are stamped and cut to size and stitched together using a serger. Fully fashioned pieces, in contrast, are knitted to the size and shape of the individual sweater components, with the shaping details as clearly visible features of the design.

Left-slanting decreases

Right-slanting decreases

Symmetrical left- and right-slanting increases

Yarn over increases

Left-slanting decreases

Yarn over increases

Right-slanting decreases

2282

Get Your Knitting into Shape: Fully Fashioned How-Tos

Knitters usually try to conceal their increases and decreases as best they can, but in fully fashioned knits we actually want to show off these details. Following are some of the essential skills every knitter should have in her or his repertoire. Later in the book, we'll explore ways to use these simple techniques to create sweaters that are beautiful, figure-flattering, and best of all, fun to knit!

Decreases

Reducing the number of stitches changes the shape of a piece of knitting and makes it narrower. Each decrease technique results in a different look. Some decreases take on the texture of knit stitches, for example; others look like purl stitches. Also, some decreases slant toward the right while others lean to the left, depending on which direction the top stitch points, since it's the most visible one. Designers often pair mirrored decreases opposite each other on a piece of knitting for a decorative effect. More on that subject later.

Knit Stitch Decreases

Knit 2 Together (decreases one stitch and slants toward the right; abbreviated k2tog)

When this method of decreasing is used, the resulting stitch leans toward the right. It's easy: Just insert the right-hand needle into two stitches at once as if they're a single stitch!

To do: With the working yarn toward the back, insert the right-hand needle from front to back, knitwise (page 151), into the first two stitches on the left-hand needle as if they were a single stitch, and wrap the yarn around the right-hand needle as you would for a knit stitch (illustration 1). Pull the yarn through both stitches, and slip both stitches off the left-hand needle at once. One stitch has been decreased, and the resulting stitch slants to the right.

[1]

Slip, Slip, Knit (decreases one stitch and slants toward the left; abbreviated ssk)

This knit decrease requires an extra step, but it creates a mirror image of the k2tog decrease described above.

To do: With the working yarn toward the back, insert the right-hand needle from the left to the right, knitwise, into the first and second stitches on the left-hand needle, *one at a time*, and slip them onto the right-hand needle (illustration 2).

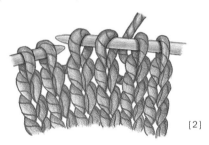

[2]

Then, insert the tip of the left-hand needle into the fronts of both slipped stitches (illustration 3) and knit them together from this position, through their back loops. One stitch has been decreased, and the resulting stitch slants to the left.

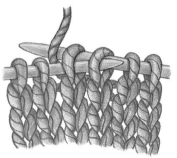

[3]

Knit 3 Together (decreases two stitches and slants toward the right; abbreviated k3tog)

This decrease is worked the same way as the k2tog decrease above, except the right-hand needle is inserted into three stitches at once, instead of two. In this case, two stitches are decreased, with the resulting stitch slanting toward the right.

Slip, Slip, Slip, Knit (decreases two stitches and slants toward the left; abbreviated sssk)

This decrease uses the same method as the ssk decrease above except three stitches are slipped rather than two stitches, one at a time, from the left-hand needle to the right-hand needle.

The usual method is to slip each of the three stitches knitwise, but some knitters prefer slipping the first stitch knitwise and the next two stitches purlwise in order to achieve a more perfect mirror image to the k3tog, as described for the modified ssk in the sidebar on page 13. It's the knitter's choice.

Purl Stitch Decreases

Purl 2 Together (decreases one stitch and slants toward the right on the knit side of the fabric; abbreviated p2tog)

This type of decrease is most often done on wrong-side rows to combine two purl stitches, mimicking the look of a k2tog on the knit side of the fabric. Sometimes, though, designers use it on the right side to cleverly decrease along a purl "valley" as in Orvieto (page 65).

To do: With the working yarn toward the front, insert the tip of the right-hand needle into the first two stitches on the left-hand needle from right to left, purlwise (page 152), as if they were a single stitch, and wrap the yarn around the right-hand needle as you would for a purl stitch (illustration 4). Pull the yarn through both stitches, then slip both stitches

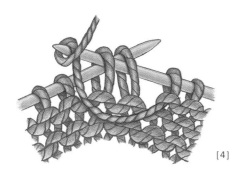

[4]

off the left-hand needle at once. One stitch has been decreased, and the resulting stitch slants to the right on the knit side of the fabric.

Slip, Slip, Purl (decreases one stitch and slants toward the left on the knit side of the fabric; abbreviated ssp)

This technique is often used on wrong-side rows to mimic the left-slanting look of the ssk decrease on the knit side of the fabric.

To do: With the working yarn toward the front, slip the first two stitches knitwise, one at a time, from the left-hand needle to the right-hand needle. Then slip these two stitches back to the left-hand needle in their twisted position. Finally, insert the tip of the right-hand needle into the back loops of these two stitches, going into the second stitch first, and then the first stitch), and purl them together *through their back loops* as if they were a single stitch (illustration 5). One stitch has been decreased, and the resulting stitch leans toward the left on the knit side of the fabric.

[5]

Purl 3 Together (abbreviated p3tog)

This decrease is worked the same as the p2tog decrease above, except the right-hand needle is inserted into three stitches at once, instead of two. Here, two stitches are decreased, with the resulting stitch slanting toward the right on the knit side of the fabric.

Slip, Slip, Slip, Purl (abbreviated sssp)

This decrease is worked the same as the ssp decrease above, except three stitches are slipped, one at a time, instead of two. Here, two stitches are decreased, the resulting stitch slanting toward the left on the knit side of the fabric.

Give It the Slip

For some knitters, the ssk decrease worked the typical way does not mirror the k2tog decrease perfectly. If you are among them and would like to make your left-leaning decrease look smoother and less like stair steps, try this method:

Slip the first stitch knitwise and the second stitch purlwise (page 152) from the left-hand needle to the right-hand needle (illustration 6). Slipping the first stitch knitwise keeps it from twisting at the bottom, producing a smoother and neater stitch; slipping the second stitch purlwise seems to help some knitters achieve a straighter, less choppy line toward the left.

Then insert the left-hand needle into the fronts of both slipped stitches (illustration 7) and knit them together from this position, through their back loops.

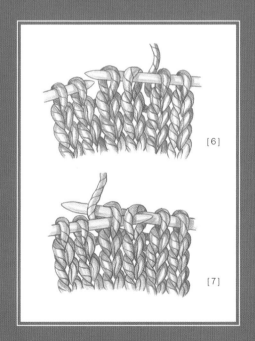

[6]

[7]

Keeping Your Directional Slants Straight

Many knitters find it difficult to remember which decrease slants which way. Here's a simple trick to help you remember which leans to the left and which leans to the right.

Write down the name of the decreases "k2tog" and "ssk." Then draw a diagonal line through the right slant in the 2 and the left slant in the s as shown. The diagonal lines match the slant of the decreases: The k2tog decrease slants to the right and the ssk decrease slants toward the left. How's that for an easy way to keep them straight?

k2tog
(Right slant)

ssk
(Left slant)

Keep It Simple

When viewed from the purl side, the p2tog decrease and the ssp decrease look surprisingly similar. Neither one slants noticeably toward the left or the right. That's why the p2tog technique is used without a matching ssp decrease in Jacqueline (page 37). Working ssp decreases to mirror the p2tog decreases isn't worth the effort in such a case. No sense slowing down the precious knitting when no one (not even the designer!) will notice the tiny detail.

Increases

Knitters have many methods for adding width to a piece of fabric. Each technique has a different effect, from making decorative holes to adding various amounts of texture, to barely there increases that are nearly invisible.

Subtle Increases

Lifted Increases

This type of increase is made by working into a stitch in the row below the stitch that is currently on the needle, and also working into the stitch the regular way. Although nearly invisible, it is handy to be able to perform the lifted increase slanting to either the left or to the right, depending on the desired effect.

To do a lifted increase slanting to the left: Insert the left-hand needle into the back of the first stitch on the right-hand needle, just below the stitch just knit (illustration 8), and knit it (illustration 9).

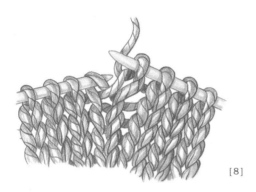

[8]

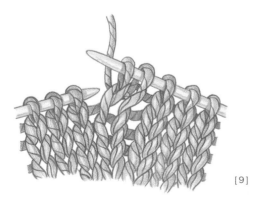

[9]

For a lifted increase slanting to the right: Knit into the back of the stitch (into its purl "bump") in the row directly below the stitch on the left-hand needle (illustration 10).

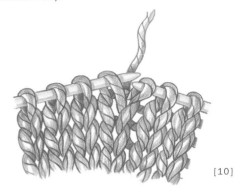

[10]

For a lifted purl increase, work the same as the knit version, except purl instead of knit. Easy!

Raised Increases (commonly known as "make one" increases)

This method of adding stitches uses the horizontal strand of yarn that hangs between the knitting needles. The knitter works into the strand, carefully twisting it to prevent a hole. As with the lifted increases above, raised increases can slant to the right and to the left. Here's how:

For a raised knit increase slanting to the left (*abbreviated M1-L*): Use the left-hand needle to scoop up the horizontal strand that's hanging between the needles *from front to back*, and knit the strand *through its back loop*, twisting it to prevent a hole in your fabric (illustration 11).

[11]

For a raised knit increase slanting to the right (*abbreviated M1-R*): Use the left-hand needle to scoop up the horizontal strand that is hanging between the needles *from back to front,* and knit the strand *through its front loop,* twisting it to prevent a hole in the work (illustration 12).

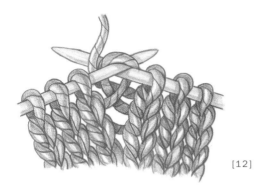

[12]

Note: If no direction is specified, use the M1-L increase.

Sometimes raised increases are worked as purl stitches, such as when increases are made on wrong-side rows as follows.

For a raised purl increase that slants to the right on the right side of the fabric: Use the left-hand needle to scoop up the horizontal strand between the needles *from back to front,* then purl the strand *through its front loop,* twisting it to prevent a hole in your fabric (illustration 13).

For a raised purl increase that slants to the left on the right side of the fabric: Use the left-hand needle to scoop up the horizontal strand between the needles *from front to back,* then purl the strand *through its back loop* (page 152), twisting it to prevent a hole in your fabric.

However, M1 purlwise increases are usually worked on right-side rows whenever a purl stitch is needed, and in these cases, the difference between left- and right-slanting stitches is hardly visible; no directional raised purl increases are necessary. Just use whichever version is easier for you.

Decorative Increases

Sometimes, especially when working fully fashioned shaping, you'll want to feature increased stitches prominently in a design. Following are some techniques.

Bar Increases

This type of increase adds a bit of horizontal texture that looks very much like a purl bump. It is easy to work and is often used when knitting ribbings, since it serves to incorporate new stitches into the pattern quickly.

To do in a knit stitch (*abbreviated k1f&b*): First, insert the right-hand needle into the indicated stitch knitwise, wrap the working yarn around the needle the regular way to knit up a stitch *but don't remove the original stitch off the left-hand needle* (illustration 14).

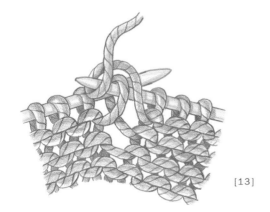

[13]

[14]

Then, reinsert your right-hand needle knitwise into the back of the same stitch, wrap the yarn around the needle to knit up a stitch (illustration 15), then slip the original stitch off. Two stitches are made out of one stitch.

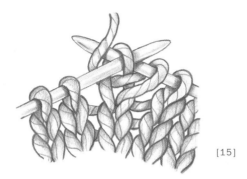

[15]

To do in a purl stitch (*abbreviated plf&b*): Insert the right-hand needle into the indicated stitch purlwise, wrap the working yarn around the regular way to purl a stitch *but don't remove the original stitch off the left-hand needle;* then, purl *through the back loop* of the same stitch; finally, slip the original stitch off the left-hand needle. Two stitches are made out of one stitch.

Yarn Over Increases

This method of increasing places an eyelet hole in the fabric just below the new stitch. The technique is different depending on whether the stitch following the yarn over is a knit or a purl stitch.

To make a yarn over before a knit stitch: Bring the working yarn to the front, between the tips of the two knitting needles (illustration 16). As you knit the next stitch, the yarn will go over the right-hand needle to create the extra stitch.

[16]

To make a yarn over before a purl stitch: Bring the working yarn to the front, between the tips of the knitting needles, and then wrap it *completely around* the right-hand needle and back to the front (illustration 17). Simply bringing the yarn to the front does not add a new stitch; the yarn must go all the way around the right-hand needle to make the increase before a purl stitch.

[17]

These increases and decreases are used in various ways throughout the projects in the book. The included Designer Workshop sections highlight many ways of including these techniques in fully fashioned shaping to create flattering knits.

Knitting as a Foreign Language: Knitting Charts 101

Charts are visual representations of knitted fabric. When I teach workshops around the country, I tell my students that the charts and symbols are just another foreign language, complete with a vocabulary list (the symbols) and syntax (the graphic layout). They're easy to translate, and using them (instead of long black-and-white paragraphs of text) will make your knitting easier, faster, and much more fun.

A Short Grammar Lesson

Charts are set up on a grid. Each square of the grid represents one stitch and each row of squares represents one row of stitches.

Because the stitch pattern is being created from the bottom up, the first row is at the bottom of the chart, and the last row is at the top.

Right-side rows are read from right to left. The following illustration shows the order in which stitches will be knit for Row 1, a right-side row, in the chart.

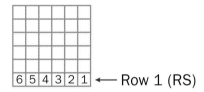

At the end of this first row, you'll flip your knitting so that the wrong side of the fabric faces you. The first stitch of a wrong-side row is the same physical stitch as the last stitch of the previous right-side row. Thus, wrong-side rows are read from left to right.

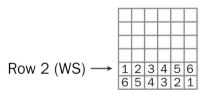

In all the patterns in this book, the first row knit is a right-side row, and so all right-side rows are odd-numbered rows. I've numbered them on the right-hand side of each chart to keep you oriented.

The Vocabulary List

Each symbol indicates the way a stitch or group of stitches will be worked; the arrangement of the symbols on the chart determines the stitch pattern.

Of course, every book and magazine seems to use a different set of symbols to represent the same knitting maneuvers. Usually, the symbols resemble the way the resulting stitches will appear once knit on the right side of the fabric. The symbol for a knit stitch, for example, is a blank box, mimicking the flat appearance of the knit stitch itself; the dot symbol for a purl stitch depicts the bumpy appearance of a purled stitch.

All rows are shown on the chart *as they appear on the public side of the fabric.* Therefore, symbols mean different things on right-side and wrong-side rows. If a symbol is used on both right- and wrong-side rows, the stitch key near the chart will tell you which knitting maneuver to use where.

Usually, wrong-side rows are pretty simple: you just knit the knit stitches and purl the purl stitches as they present themselves to you on the knitting needle. Many students in my classes call them "rest rows"! Scan the entire chart before you begin to see if that's the case. If so, you can zip along those wrong-side rows reading your knitting rather than the chart!

In some charts, bold vertical lines indicate the stitch repeat, and if extra stitches are required on each side to center the pattern on the fabric, they are shown to the left and right of the repeat.

Glossary of Symbols

□ = K on RS; p on WS

· = P on RS; k on WS

▨ = No stitch

ℚ = K *through back loop* on RS; p *through back loop* on WS

o = Yarn over

⟋ = K2tog on RS; p2tog on WS

⟍ = Ssk on RS; ssp on WS

⟍ = P2tog on RS; k2tog on WS

⟋ = Ssp on RS; ssk on WS

⋀ = Slip 2 sts at once knitwise; k1; p2sso

⋏ = Insert needle into the 2nd and 1st sts as if to p2tog through back loops; slip these 2 sts onto the RH needle in this position; p1; p2sso

⤬ = Right Twist = Slip next st onto cn and hold in back; k1; k1 from cn **OR** k2tog, leaving them on LH needle; insert point of RH needle between these 2 sts and k the first one again

⤬ = Left Twist = Slip next st onto cn and hold in front; k1; k1 from cn **OR** skip first st and k next st *in back loop*; then k the skipped st; slip both sts off LH needle together

K = Knot = K into (front, back, front) of next st, turn; p3, turn; slip 2 sts at once knitwise, k1, p2sso

= Slip next st onto cn and hold in back; k next st *through back loop*; p1 from cn

= Slip next st onto cn and hold in front; p1; k1 from cn *through back loop*

= Slip next st onto cn and hold in back; k2; p1 from cn

= Slip 2 sts onto cn and hold in front; p1; k2 from cn

= Slip 2 sts onto cn and hold in back; k2; k2 from cn

= Slip 2 sts onto cn and hold in front; k2; k2 from cn

= Slip 2 sts onto cn and hold in back; k2; p2 from cn

= Slip 2 sts onto cn and hold in front; p2; k2 from cn

= Slip next st onto cn and hold in back; k3; p1 from cn

= Slip 3 sts onto cn and hold in front; p1; k3 from cn

= Slip 2 sts onto cn and hold in back; k3; p2 from cn

= Slip 3 sts onto cn and hold in front; p2; k3 from cn

= Slip 3 sts onto cn and hold in back; k3; k3 from cn

= Slip 3 sts onto cn and hold in front; k3; k3 from cn

Abbreviations

Following is a list of abbreviations used in the projects and charts of this book. Many of the techniques are discussed in the General Knitting Techniques section (page 149).

beg	beg(inning)
cm	centimeter(s)
cn	cable needle
g	gram(s)
k	knit
k1f&b	knit into the front and back of a stitch (increase)
k1-tbl	knit next stitch through its back loop
k2tog	knit the next 2 stitches together; this is a right-slanting decrease
k3tog	knit the next 3 stitches together; this is a right-slanting double decrease
LH	left-hand
MB	Make a bobble
m	meter(s)
mm	millimeter(s)
M1	make 1 (increase)
M1-L	make 1 left (increase)
M1-R	make 1 right (increase)
oz	ounce(s)
p	purl
p1b&f	purl into back and front of a stitch (increase)
p1-tbl	purl next stitch through its back loop
p2sso	pass 2 slipped stitches over
p2tog	purl the next 2 stitches together; this is a right-slanting decrease
RH	right-hand
rnd(s)	round(s)
rpt	repeat
RS	right side (of work)

s2kp2	centered double decrease = slip next 2 stitches at once knitwise, knit the next stitch, pass the 2 slipped stitches over the knit stitch
ssk	slip the next 2 stitches knitwise, one at a time from the left-hand needle to the right-hand one, insert the left-hand needle tip into the fronts of both slipped stitches to knit them together from this position; this is a left-slanting decrease
ssp	slip the next 2 stitches knitwise, one at a time from the left-hand needle to the right-hand one, return both stitches to left-hand needle and insert the right-hand needle into them from left to right and from back to front, to purl them together through their back loops; this is a left-slanting decrease
sssk	slip the next 3 stitches knitwise, one at a time from the left-hand needle to the right-hand one, insert the left-hand needle tip into the fronts of all three slipped stitches to knit them together from this position; this is a left-slanting double decrease
sssp	slip the next 3 stitches knitwise, one at a time from the left-hand needle to the right-hand one, return all three stitches to left-hand needle and insert the right-hand needle into them from left to right and from back to front, to purl them together through their back loops; this is a left-slanting double decrease
st(s)	stitch(es)
WS	wrong side (of work)
yd(s)	yard(s)
*	repeat instructions after asterisk or between the asterisks across the row or for as many times as instructed
( )	alternate measurements and/or instructions for different sizes; also, repeat the instructions within parentheses for as many times as instructed
[ ]	repeat the instructions within bracket for as many times as instructed; these brackets also indicate the separation between imperial and metric measurements in the pattern text

Knitting to Flatter
Often, knitters are attracted to sweater projects that look fun and interesting to knit but forget that the final product must be wearable and, hopefully, flattering. Obviously, not every garment is appropriate for everyone. Here's how to determine your figure type and choose the designs best suited to you.

Body Type

Most women's bodies fall into five basic shapes: triangle, inverted triangle, round, rectangle, or hourglass. What shape are you?

First, you'll need to take some body measurements. It's best to do so while wearing a good, supportive bra, and it's probably a smart idea to enlist a friend to help you, so you're sure the measuring tool doesn't dip down in the back, giving you inaccurate measurements.

Also, since we tend to subconsciously round our measurements up or down, I suggest that all measurements be taken using a length of nonstretchy yarn or ribbon and then use a ruler. Linen or mercerized cotton yarn is best; stay away from most wools and silks.

Measure your bust at its fullest area, your waist at its narrowest spot (usually just above the navel), and your hips and rear end at their fullest spot, keeping the yarn close to the body but not too tight or too loose. It's the ratio of these three measurements to each other that determines body type, as shown in the table opposite.

Each project in this book is designed to flatter specific body types, so be sure to look for the body shape icons for each pattern in this book. And the entire Designer Workshop in chapter 4 (page 100) is devoted to ways to make every figure type look great. After all, the goal is to design garments that have designer details which are not only fun to knit, but flattering as well.

Fit

Ease is the difference between the actual measurements of the finished garment and your physical body measurements. More ease provides a roomier fit; less ease creates a tighter fit. Negative ease describes a sweater that is smaller than the body; the fabric is meant to stretch to fit to create flattering, body-conscious lines.

Here are the fits and eases referred to in the projects in this book.

Very close-fitting: Actual body measurements or smaller (negative ease)

Close-fitting: Actual body measurement + 1–2"/ [2.5–5cm]

Standard-fitting: Actual body measurement + 2–4"/ [5–10cm]

Loose-fitting: Actual body measurement + 4–6"/ [10–15cm]

Oversized: Actual body measurement + 6"/[15cm] or more

SHAPE ICON	Body Type	Relative relationship between physical measurements	Wardrobe Tips	Sweater Dos	Sweater Don'ts
▲	Triangle	Hip measurement larger than both waist and bust	Distract attention from the hips; emphasize the chest and neckline	Interesting necklines; pattern interest in the upper third of the design	Close-fitting ribbings at hips; strong horizontal lines in the lower third of the design; tops that end at the widest place on the hips
▼	Inverted Triangle	Bust measurement larger than both waist and hips	Distract attention from shoulder and upper body; draw attention to slender hips and waist	Set-in sleeves, deep necklines; interesting stitch patterns in the lower half of the design; flared silhouettes	Heavy drop shoulders; giant lapels or collars; puffed sleeves
●	Round	Waist measurement larger than both hips and bust	De-emphasize the waist	Empire waists; deep necklines or other design details in the upper third of sweaters	Boxy silhouettes; high necklines; heavy cabled fabrics
■	Rectangle	Hip, waist, and bust measurements are just about equal	Create the illusion of curves	Cinch in the waist; add bust darts; define the shoulders and upper body area; flowy, feminine A-line silhouettes	Boxy silhouettes
⧓	Hourglass	Hip and bust measurements are relatively equal, with a much narrower waist measurement	Highlight curves	Add waist shaping; belted looks	Loose, straight silhouettes

2

Step Away from the Edge

Typically, knitters go to great lengths to make their increases and decreases as invisible as possible. (Could this be because they haven't effectively perfected their technique?) Fully fashioned shaping, a technique used in the fashion industry, deliberately puts these elements on display, creating exquisite garments that are beautiful and polished-looking.

Designer Workshop

Making Simple Stockinette Garments
Look Extraordinary

As we discovered in chapter 1, knitters have several methods to choose from when shaping garments. Each technique adds a different design element to a piece of knitting, especially when worked in a fully fashioned way. Let's start exploring the options.

Fully fashioned shaping occurs when increases and decreases are worked one or two—and sometimes even more!—stitches away from the edge of the fabric.

This designer approach creates a frame, usually stockinette, which outlines the shape of the piece of fabric. This easy technique—simply moving the increases and decreases toward the interior of the knitting—adds a vertical element to the garment. Placed near side seams, these vertical lines draw the eye up and have a slimming effect; used along raglan seams, the lines point toward the face, putting the focus where you want it (and away from where you don't).

And, without the extra bulk and fabric strain often experienced when shaping is worked right at the edge of garments, seams are neater and easier to sew, since the increases and decreases are moved away from selvedge edges. Bonus!

Fully fashioned shaping can also make your conventional neckbands easier to finish, since stitches are more easily picked up between plain stockinette stitches rather than along awkwardly shaped decreased edges. Simply put, smoother edges make for neater finishing.

Of course, even if a pattern doesn't specifically call for fully fashioned increases and decreases, you can add them yourself! It will make the difference between an ordinary sweater and a knockout.

Decreases the Fully Fashioned Way

Choose one of the following methods of decreasing, depending on the effect you'd like to achieve.

Increases and decreases that slant with the shape of the fabric will blend in, creating an organic look to your design; for highest contrast, you'll want to choose ones that slant against the grain of the fabric.

Smooth Lines

Placing left-slanting decreases on the right-hand side of the fabric and right-slanting ones on the left-hand side creates subtle and neat vertical lines along the edges. The swatch shows mirrored decreases worked this way. Here, a left-slanting ssk decrease (page 11) is used to combine the fifth and sixth stitches on the right-hand side and a right-slanting k2tog decrease (page 11) is used to combine the fifth and sixth stitches on the left-hand side. Each decrease is leaning toward the interior of the fabric, leaving a subtle stockinette stitch frame on the outer edges. Aster Stripes (page 33) uses smooth fully fashioned decreases worked one stitch away from the edge.

When your main fabric has a pattern stitch, it's often a good idea to work all shaping with smooth fully fashioned lines. If you keep the first 4 stitches (or 2 or 10 or whatever) in plain stockinette, you'll decrease or increase just inside the stockinette frame you're creating. Then, once you have enough stitches for a full repeat of your stitch pattern, it will be simple to incorporate the new stitches into pattern. Easy!

Swatch It Up

Give it a try! Here's how to knit a sample with smooth fully fashioned decreases: cast on 35 stitches. Begin stockinette, and work a decrease row every 4 rows until 21 stitches remain.

If your Decrease Row is worked on the right side: K4, ssk, knit to the last 6 stitches, k2tog, k4.

If your Decrease Row is worked on the wrong side: P4, p2tog, purl to the last 6 stitches, ssp, p4.

One stitch has been decreased each side of the Decrease Row; two stitches have been decreased each row in total.

Feathered Lines

When the decreases slant *away from the interior* of the fabric and toward the sides, another effect is achieved. The swatch below shows right-slanting k2tog decreases on the right-hand side of the fabric and left-slanting ssk decreases on the left-hand side, each worked five stitches in from the edge. Here, the decreases appear as little diagonal "blips" pointing away from center. They're a focal point of the fabric. Feathered decreases are used in Aberdeen (page 49) for a very different reason: it's easier to maintain the color pattern when decreasing this way.

Swatch It Up

Try it yourself. To knit a sample swatch with feathered fully fashioned decreases: Cast on 35 stitches. Begin stockinette, and work a decrease row every 4 rows until 21 stitches remain.

If your Decrease Row is worked on the right side: K4, k2tog, knit to the last 6 stitches, ssk, k4.

If your Decrease Row is worked on the wrong side: P4, ssp, purl to the last 6 stitches, p2tog, p4.

One stitch has been decreased each side of the Decrease Row.

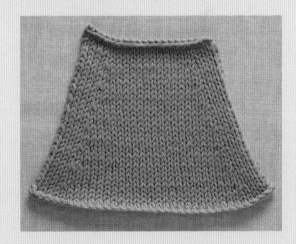

Living on the Edge

Of course, fully fashioned decreasing describes any time shaping is worked away from the selvedges, but different effects are achieved depending where the decreases are positioned relative to the edge of the fabric. The swatch on page 25 (left) shows smooth decreases worked five stitches from the edge. For comparison, the top swatch on this page has the mirrored decreases worked three stitches in, and the bottom swatch shows them placed seven stitches in. The former will have a subtle effect while in the latter, the shaping will become the forefront of the design. Like most things in knitting, it's fun (and useful) to be able to choose the effect you want.

Increases the Fully Fashioned Way

As with decreasing, knitters have the choice of several different methods for increasing, from quite subtle to more decorative and ornate.

Directional Stranded Increases
(commonly known as M1 increases)

To add stitches while affecting the tension or texture of stitches that are already on the needles in a very subtle way, stranded increases are usually used. This type of increase borrows a bit of yarn from the stitches on either side of the new stitch. Different effects are achieved when the increases lean toward the selvedge edges or toward the center of the fabric. Let's take a look:

The swatch above shows directional M1 increases (page 14) slanting *toward* the interior of the fabric. Here, M1-L is worked near the beginning of rows, and M1-R is worked near the end of rows. Notice how the stockinette frame going up the sides appears distinct from the main part of the knitting. Fully fashioned increases are worked this way in Aster Stripes (page 33).

On the other hand, the swatch on the right shows what happens when M1 increases slant toward the selvedge edges. In this case, the little diagonal "blips" formed by the increases slant with the grain of the fabric, blending in.

Swatch It Up

Try it! To knit a sample with stranded increases, cast on 21 stitches. Begin stockinette, and work an increase row every 4 rows until 35 stitches are on the needle.

For a strong effect (see swatch, above left):
If your Increase Row is worked on the right side: K4, M1-L, knit to the last 4 stitches, M1-R, k4.

If your Increase Row is worked on the wrong side: P4, M1-R purlwise (page 15), purl to the last 4 stitches, M1-L purlwise (page 15), p4.

One stitch is increased on each side of the Increase Row.

For a subtle effect (see swatch, above right):
If your Increase Row is worked on the right side: K4, M1-R, knit to the last 4 stitches, M1-L, k4.

If your Increase Row is worked on the wrong side: P4, M1-L purlwise, purl to the last 4 stitches, M1-R purlwise, p4.

One stitch has been increased on each side of the Increase Row.

Of course, it is the knitter's choice which version to use, depending on the desired effect. The important thing is that all M1 increases slant toward one direction on one edge of the fabric and toward the other direction on the other edge. Stacking the increases this way adds a cohesive look to a design.

Decorative Yarn Over Increases

Using a yarn over increase (page 16) a few stitches in from the side selvedges makes a delicate line of holes that can accentuate the shape of the knit piece.

The swatch above shows this type of increase worked 4 stitches away from the edges.

Although yarn over increases are not directional increases, when abutted next to each other as in a seam, they're quite beautiful. The swatch on the right shows fully fashioned yarn over increases worked on either side of a seam.

Swatch It Up

Give it a go! To knit a sample with fully fashioned yarn over increases, cast on 21 stitches. Begin stockinette, and work an increase row every 4 rows until 35 stitches are on the needle. This method is best used 2 or more stitches away from the edge.

If your Increase Row is worked on the right side: K4, yarn over, knit to the last 4 stitches, yarn over, k4. One stitch has been increased each side.

If your Increase Row is worked on the wrong side: P4, yarn over, purl to the last 4 stitches, yarn over, p4. One stitch has been increased each side.

Note that it is important to always wrap the working yarn around the right-hand needle in the same direction each time: in between the tips of the two knitting needles toward the front, then up around the top of the right-hand needle to the back. Wrapping the yarn around the needle in the opposite direction creates a smaller hole.

In Fine Feather

For more dramatic feathered decreases, work paired *double* decreases. Use the right-slanting k3tog (page 12) on the right-hand side of the fabric and the left-slanting sssk (page 12) on the left-hand side for symmetry. The swatch below shows double feathered decreases. Notice how even though the shaping is worked every 8 rows (instead of every 4 rows as in the previous examples), those little diagonal blips truly stand out and become a design element of their own.

Of course, fully fashioned details show up really well on either side of a seam. The swatch on the right reveals the beauty of double feathered decreases mirrored along a seam. Here, the left-slanting sssk decrease and the right-slanting k3tog decrease each point toward the center seamline. Imagine how dramatic this technique would look along the diagonal line of a raglan!

Swatch It Up

Give it a whirl! To knit a sample with double feathered fully fashioned decreases, cast on 35 stitches. Begin stockinette, and work a decrease row every 8 rows until 19 stitches remain. This method is best used 3 or more stitches away from the edge.

If your Decrease Row is worked on the right side: K4, k3tog, knit to the last 7 stitches, sssk, k4.

If your Decrease Row is worked on the wrong side: P4, sssp, purl to the last 7 stitches, p3tog, p4.

Two stitches have been decreased each side of each Decrease Row—that's four stitches decreased each row.

Lifted Increases

Lifted increases (page 14) pull up stitches from the row below and can lean toward the left or right, just like stranded increases. Different looks are achieved depending on which way the new stitches slant.

The swatch above shows left-leaning lifted increases near the beginning of rows and right-leaning ones near the end of rows.

The swatch on the right shows the increases reversed, with the right-leaning ones near the beginning of rows and the left-leaning ones near the end.

It's the knitter's choice which way to go, but it is essential to be consistent once the line is set up.

Swatch It Up

Try it! To knit a sample with mirrored fully fashioned lifted increases, cast on 21 stitches. Begin stockinette, and work an increase row every 4 rows until 35 stitches are on the needle.

For an Increase Row with left-slanting increases near the beginning of rows and right-slanting ones near the end of rows: K4, make a left-slanting lifted increase, knit to the last 4 stitches, make a right-slanting lifted increase, k4. One stitch has been increased each side.

For an Increase Row with right-slanting increases near the beginning of rows and left-slanting ones near the end of rows: K4, make a right-slanting lifted increase, knit to the last 4 stitches, make a left-slanting lifted increase, k4. One stitch has been increased each side.

Beaded Increases

Worked 2 or more stitches away from the selvedge, this type of increase creates tiny textured dots that sit on top of the fabric. The increases are made by purling and knitting into a single stitch.

The swatch opposite (top left) shows beaded increases worked 4 stitches away from the edge.

These increases are beautiful worked on either side of a seam, as seen in the swatch opposite (center left). As a bonus, the purl bumps are easy to see, which makes it easier to keep track of how many increases have been worked.

Swatch It Up

Check it out! To knit a sample with fully fashioned beaded increases, cast on 21 stitches. Begin stockinette, and work an increase row every 4 rows until 35 stitches are on the needle.

If your Increase Row is worked on the right side: K4, [knit and then purl] into the next stitch, knit to the last 5 stitches, [purl and then knit] into the next stitch, k4.

If your Increase Row is worked on the wrong side: P4, [purl and then knit] into the next stitch, purl to the last 5 stitches, [knit and then purl] into the next stitch, p4.

A Variation on Beaded Increases

Knitters can use bar increases (page 15) to create neat fully fashioned increases. Like the previous example, two stitches are worked into a single stitch, but in this case, the increase is made by knitting into the front and then the back of a stitch (see swatch above). Because the two new stitches are made in different "legs" of the original stitch, the yarn is stretched less, yielding a neater result.

For symmetrical increases, be sure to work the bar increases one stitch closer to the edge on the right edge of the fabric.

Swatch It Up

 Go for it! To knit a sample of this variation on beaded increases, cast on 21 stitches. Begin stockinette and work an increase row every 4 rows until 35 stitches are on the needle.

If your Increase Row is worked on the right side: K4, [knit into the front and then the back] of the next stitch, knit to the last 6 stitches, [knit into the front and then the back] of the next stitch, k5.

If your Increase Row is worked on the wrong side: P4, [purl into the front and then the back] of the next stitch, purl to the last 6 stitches, [purl into the front and then the back] of the next stitch, p5.

In this example, the textured "blip" is five stitches in from the edge on each side.

Be sure to experiment with each of these different fully fashioned increases and decreases so you can choose which ones you'd like to incorporate in your next knitting project. Just because a pattern doesn't specify this sort of detail doesn't mean you can't add it!

Aster Stripes

This sporty wardrobe basic makes a great layering piece with its tapered, flattering silhouette and a high, ribbed turtleneck. It's the perfect choice as an in-between season essential. Of course, if you prefer a crewneck, work your neckband for 1"/[2.5cm] and then bind off. Basic knit and purl decreases are used in the design, making it a good opportunity to practice fully fashioned shaping!

Skill Level
Advanced Beginner

Sizes
Small (Medium, Large, 1X, 2X, 3X, 4X). Instructions are for the smallest size, with changes for other sizes noted in parentheses as necessary.

Finished Measurements
Bust: 32 (36, 40, 44, 48, 52, 56)"/[81 (91, 101.5, 112, 122, 132, 142)cm]
Length: 23 (23½, 24, 24, 24½, 24½, 25)"/[58.5 (59.5, 61, 61, 62, 62, 63.5)cm]

Materials
- Cascade Yarns' *Ultra Pima* (3-light/DK weight; 100% pima cotton; each approximately 3½ oz/[100g] and 220 yds/[200m]): 2 (3, 3, 4, 4, 4, 5) hanks of Orchid #3709 (A), 1 (2, 2, 2, 2, 3, 3) hanks of Spring Moss #3745 (B), 1 (1, 1, 1, 1, 1, 2) hanks of Chartreuse #3746 (C), 2 (2, 2, 2, 2, 2, 3) hanks of Iris #3708 (D), and 1 (1, 1, 1, 1, 1, 2) hanks of Buttercup #3748 (E) Light
- Size 3 (3.25mm) knitting needles
- Size 5 (3.75mm) knitting needles or size needed to obtain gauge
- Blunt-end yarn needle

Gauge
22 stitches and 30 rows = 4"/[10cm] in stockinette stitch with the larger needles.
To save time, take time to check gauge.

Stitch Patterns
Rib Pattern (*multiple of 4 + 2 stitches*)
ROW 1 (RS): K2, *p2, k2; repeat from the * across.
ROW 2: P2, *k2, p2; repeat from the * across.
Repeat Rows 1 and 2 for the pattern.

Stockinette Stitch (*any number of stitches*)
ROW 1 (RS): Knit across.
ROW 2: Purl across.
Repeat Rows 1 and 2 for pattern.

Stripe Pattern (*over 64 rows*)

Working in stockinette stitch, work 8 rows *each* of *B, C, A, D, B, E, D, A; repeat from the * for the pattern.

Notes

- The instructions include 1 selvedge stitch on each side; these stitches are not included in the finished measurements.
- For fully fashioned armhole and sleeve cap decreases: On right-side rows, k1, ssk, knit to the last 3 stitches, k2tog, k1; on wrong-side rows, p3, p2tog, purl to the last 5 stitches, ssp, p3.
- For fully fashioned neck decreases: On the right-hand side of the neck, knit to 3 stitches before the neck edge, k2tog, k1; on the left-hand side of the neck, k1, ssk, knit to the end of the row.
- For fully fashioned increases: On right-side rows, k4, M1-L (page 14), knit to the last 4 stitches, M1-R, k4; on wrong-side rows, p4, M1 purlwise (page 15), purl to the last 4 stitches, M1 purlwise, p4.
- For sweater assembly, refer to the illustration for set-in construction on page 158.

Back

With the smaller needles and A, cast on 82 (90, 102, 114, 124, 134, 146) stitches.

Begin the Rib Pattern, and work even until the piece measures approximately 3¼"/[8.5cm] from the beginning, ending after a wrong-side row, and on the last row, use the M1 purlwise technique (page 15) to increase 0 (1, 1, 0, 1, 1, 1) stitch after the first stitch and before the last stitch of the last row—82 (92, 104, 114, 126, 136, 148) stitches.

Change to the larger needles and B; begin stockinette stitch and the Stripe Pattern, and work fully fashioned increases (see Notes) each side every 6 rows 4 times—90 (100, 112, 122, 134, 144, 156) stitches.

Continue even until the piece measures approximately 14½"/[37cm] from the beginning, ending after a wrong-side row. *Make a note of which row of the Stripe Pattern you ended with.*

SHAPE ARMHOLES

Bind off 4 (5, 6, 8, 9, 11, 12) stitches at the beginning of the next 2 rows; bind off 2 (3, 4, 4, 5, 5, 6) stitches at the beginning of the next 2 rows, then work fully fashioned decreases (see Notes) every row 0 (0, 2, 4,

8, 12, 16) times, every other row 0 (3, 5, 6, 5, 3, 2) times, then every 4 rows 3 (2, 1, 0, 0, 0, 0) times— 72 (74, 76, 78, 80, 82, 84) stitches remain.

Continue even until the piece measures approximately 21½ (22, 22½, 22½, 23, 23, 23½)"/[54.5 (56, 57, 57, 58.5, 58.5, 59.5)cm] from the beginning, ending after a wrong-side row.

SHAPE NECK

K19 (20, 21, 22, 23, 24, 25), join a second ball of yarn and bind off the middle 34 stitches, knit to the end of the row.

Working both sides at once with separate balls of yarn, work fully fashioned neck decreases (see Notes) on the next right-side row—18 (19, 20, 21, 22, 23, 24) stitches remain each side.

Work both sides even with separate balls of yarn until the piece measures approximately 22 (22½, 23, 23, 23½, 24)"/[56 (57, 58.5, 58.5, 59.5, 61)cm] from the beginning, ending after a wrong-side row.

SHAPE SHOULDERS

Bind off 4 (5 5, 5, 5, 6, 6) stitches at the beginning of the next 6 rows, then bind off 6 (4, 5, 6, 7, 5, 6) stitches at the beginning of the next 2 rows.

Front

Work the same as the Back until the piece measures approximately 20 (20½, 21, 21, 21½, 21½, 22)"/ [51 (52, 53.5, 53.5, 54.5, 54.5, 56)cm] from the beginning, ending after a wrong-side row.

SHAPE NECK

K29 (30, 31, 32, 33, 34, 35); join a second ball of yarn and bind off the middle 14 stitches, knit to the end of the row.

Working both sides at once with separate balls of yarn, bind off 5 stitches at each neck edge once; bind off 3 stitches at each neck edge once; work fully fashioned neck decreases (see Notes) at each neck edge every right-side row 3 times—18 (19, 20, 21, 22, 23, 24) stitches remain each side.

Continue even until the piece measures the same as the Back to the shoulders.

SHAPE SHOULDERS

Work same as for the Back.

Sleeves (Make 2)

With the smaller needles and A, cast on 58 (58, 62, 62, 66, 66, 74) stitches.

Begin the Rib Pattern, and work even until the piece measures approximately 1"/[2.5cm] from the beginning, ending after a wrong-side row.

Change to the larger needles and B; begin stockinette stitch and the Stripe Pattern, and work fully fashioned sleeve increases (see Notes) each side every row 0 (0, 0, 0, 2, 8, 6) times, every other row 0 (2, 2, 8, 7, 4, 5) times, every 4 rows 1 (3, 3, 0, 0, 0, 0) times, then every 6 rows 2 (0, 0, 0, 0, 0, 0) times—64 (68, 72, 78, 84, 90, 96) stitches.

Continue even until the piece measures approximately 4"/[10cm] from the beginning, ending after the same row of the Stripe Pattern as the Front and Back to the armholes.

SHAPE CAP

Bind off 4 (5, 6, 8, 9, 11, 12) stitches at the beginning of the next 2 rows; work fully fashioned sleeve cap decreases (see Notes) each side every 4 rows 2 (3, 4, 3, 3, 2, 2) times, then every other row 13 (13, 13, 15, 17, 19, 21) times—26 stitches remain.

Bind off 2 stitches at the beginning of the next 4 rows—18 stitches remain.

Bind off.

Finishing

Darn in all remaining yarn tails (page 156).

Block all pieces to the finished measurements (page 156).

Sew the left shoulder seam.

Neckband

With right side facing, smaller needles, and A, pick up and knit 110 stitches around the neck.

Begin the Rib Pattern, and work even until the neckband measures approximately 9"/[23cm] from the beginning, or to the desired length.

Bind off in the pattern.

Sew the right shoulder seam, including the side of the neckband.

Set in the sleeves.

Sew the sleeve seams.

Sew the side seams.

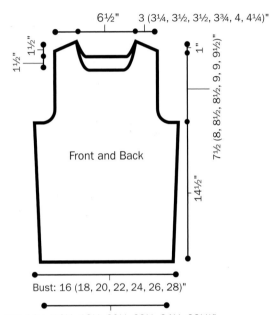

6½"   3 (3¼, 3½, 3½, 3¾, 4, 4¼)"

1½"

1½"

1"

7½ (8, 8½, 8½, 9, 9, 9½)"

14½"

Front and Back

Bust: 16 (18, 20, 22, 24, 26, 28)"

Hip: 14½ (16½, 18½, 20½, 22½, 24½, 26½)"

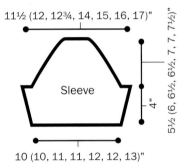

11½ (12, 12¾, 14, 15, 16, 17)"

5½ (6, 6½, 6½, 7, 7, 7½)"

4"

Sleeve

10 (10, 11, 11, 12, 12, 13)"

Jacqueline

Knit this classic jacket for the office and beyond. Since the fabric is reverse stockinette, purl decreases and increases create the shaping details.

Skill Level
Intermediate

Sizes
Small (Medium, Large, 1X, 2X, 3X). Instructions are for the smallest size, with changes for other sizes noted in parentheses as necessary.

Finished Measurements
Bust (*buttoned*): 34½ (38½, 42½, 46½, 50½, 54½)"/[87.5 (98, 108, 118, 128.5, 138.5)cm]
Length: 21½ (21½, 22, 22½, 23, 23)"/[54.5 (54.5, 56, 57, 58.5, 58.5)cm]

Materials
- Knit One Crochet Too's *Wrapunzel* (4-medium/worsted weight; 70% super-wash wool/30% acrylic; each approximately 1¾ oz/[50g] and 93 yds/[85m]): 10 (11, 12, 13, 14, 15) balls of Poppy Gold #411   Medium
- Size 6 (4mm) knitting needles
- Size 8 (5mm) knitting needles or size needed to obtain gauge
- 4 stitch holders
- 5 (5, 5, 5, 6, 6) stitch markers
- 5 (5, 5, 5, 6, 6) buttons, 1¼"/[32mm] (JHB International's *Stitched Wave Style #83119* buttons were used on sample garment)
- Blunt-end yarn needle
- Pointed sewing needle

Gauge
17 stitches and 24 rows = 4"/[10cm] in reverse stockinette stitch with the larger needles.
To save time, take time to check gauge.

Stitch Patterns
Seed Stitch (*multiple of 2 + 1 stitches*)
ROW 1 (RS): K1, *p1, k1; repeat from the * across.
PATTERN ROW: As Row 1.

Reverse Stockinette Stitch (*any number of stitches*)
ROW 1 (RS): Purl across.
ROW 2: Knit across.
Repeat Rows 1 and 2 for the pattern.

Back

With the smaller needles, cast on 73 (81, 89, 97, 107, 115) stitches.

Begin working seed stitch, and work even until the piece measures approximately 1"/[2.5cm] from the beginning, ending after a wrong-side row.

Change to the larger needles; begin reverse stockinette stitch, and work even until the piece measures approximately 2½"/[6.5cm] from the beginning, ending after a wrong-side row.

DECREASE FOR WAIST

Work fully fashioned decreases (see Notes) each side on the next row, then every 8 rows 3 more times—65 (73, 81, 89, 99, 107) stitches remain.

Continue even until the piece measures approximately 8"/[20.5cm] from the beginning, ending after a wrong-side row.

INCREASE FOR BUST

Work fully fashioned increases (see Notes) each side on the next row, then every other row 3 more times— 73 (81, 89, 97, 107, 115) stitches.

Continue even until the piece measures approximately 12½"/[32cm] from the beginning, ending after a wrong-side row.

SHAPE ARMHOLES

Bind off 4 (5, 6, 7, 8, 9) stitches at the beginning of the next 2 rows, bind off 2 (3, 3, 4, 4, 5) stitches at the beginning of the next 2 rows, then work fully fashioned decreases (see Notes) each side every other row 1 (1, 2, 1, 4, 4) times, then every 4 rows 2 (2, 2, 3, 2, 2) times—55 (59, 63, 67, 71, 75) stitches remain.

Continue even until the piece measures approximately 20½ (20½, 21, 21½, 22, 22)"/[52 (52, 53.5, 54.5, 56, 56)cm] from the beginning, ending after a wrong-side row.

SHAPE SHOULDERS

Bind off 5 (5, 6, 7, 8, 8) stitches at the beginning of the next 4 rows, then bind off 5 (7, 7, 7, 7, 9) stitches at the beginning of the next 2 rows—25 stitches remain.

Bind off.

Notes

- For fully fashioned decreases on the Back and sleeve caps: On right-side rows, p2, p2tog, purl to the last 4 stitches, p2tog, p2.
- For fully fashioned decreases on the Left Front: On right-side rows, p2, p2tog, work in the established pattern to the end; on wrong-side rows, work in the established pattern to the last 4 stitches, k2tog, k2.
- For fully fashioned decreases on the Right Front: On right-side rows, work in the established pattern to the last 4 stitches, p2tog, p2; on wrong-side rows, k2, k2tog, work in the established pattern to the end.
- For fully fashioned increases: p2, M1 purlwise (page 15), work to the last 2 stitches, M1 purlwise, p2.
- Make buttonholes on the Right Front opposite markers on right-side rows as follows: Work 2 stitches in seed stitch, bind off 3 stitches purlwise, work in pattern to the end of the row; on the subsequent row, use the cable cast-on method (page 149) to cast on 3 stitches above the bound-off stitches of the previous row.
- For sweater assembly, refer to the illustration for set-in construction on page 158.

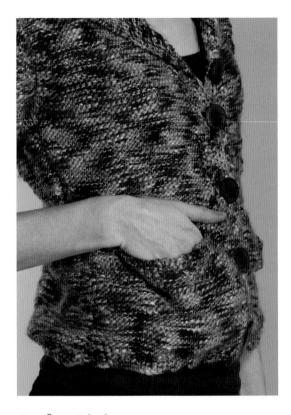

Pocket Linings (Make 2)

With the larger needles, cast on 21 sts.

Begin reverse stockinette stitch, and work even until the piece measures approximately 4½"/[11.5cm] from the beginning, ending after a wrong-side row.

Slip the stitches onto a holder.

Left Front

With the smaller needles, cast on 41 (45, 49, 53, 57, 61) stitches.

Begin working seed stitch; work even until the piece measures approximately 1"/[2.5cm] from the beginning, ending after a wrong-side row.

Change to the larger needles; work reverse stockinette stitch to the last 7 stitches, then continue seed stitch across 7 stitches.

Continue even in the established patterns until the piece measures approximately 2½"/[6.5cm] from the beginning, ending after a wrong-side row.

DECREASE FOR WAIST

Work fully fashioned decreases (see Notes) at the armhole edge on the next row, then every 8 rows 3 more times, *and at the same time,* when 38 (42, 46, 50, 54, 58) stitches remain and the piece measures approximately 5½"/[14cm] from the beginning, place the pocket lining as follows on a right-side row: P8 (10, 13, 15, 17, 19), slip the next 21 stitches onto a holder, purl across 21 stitches from pocket lining holder (with the purl side up), work to the end of the row.

Once all waist decreases are completed, 37 (41, 45, 49, 53, 57) stitches remain.

Continue even until the piece measures approximately 8"/[20.5cm] from the beginning, ending after a wrong-side row.

INCREASE FOR BUST

Work fully fashioned increases (see Notes) at the armhole edge on the next row, then every other row 3 more times—41 (45, 49, 53, 57, 61) stitches.

Continue even until the piece measures approximately 12½"/[32cm] from the beginning, ending after a wrong-side row.

SHAPE ARMHOLE

Bind off 4 (5, 6, 7, 8, 9) stitches at the armhole edge once, bind off 2 (3, 3, 4, 4, 5) stitches at the armhole edge once, then work fully fashioned decreases (see Notes) at the armhole edge every other row 1 (1, 2, 1, 4, 4) times, then every 4 rows 2 (2, 2, 3, 2, 2) times, *and at the same time,* when the piece measures approximately 13½ (13½, 14, 14½, 15, 15)"/[34.5 (34.5, 35.5, 37, 38, 38)cm] from the beginning, ending after a wrong-side row, place a marker between the seed stitch buttonband and the reverse stockinette stitches, and shape the lapel as follows:

SHAPE LAPEL

LAPEL INCREASE ROW (RS): Work to the marker, slip the marker, M1 knitwise or purlwise as needed to maintain the seed stitch pattern, work in seed stitch to the end of the row.

Repeat the Lapel Increase Row every 10 rows 3 more times, working new stitches in seed stitch as they accumulate—36 (38, 40, 42, 43, 45) stitches.

Remove the marker, and continue even until the piece measures approximately 18½ (18½, 19, 19½, 20,

20)"/[47 (47, 48.5, 49.5, 51, 51)cm] from the beginning, ending after a right-side row.

SHAPE NECK
Bind off 8 (8, 8, 8, 7, 7) stitches at the beginning of the next row, then bind off 6 stitches at the neck edge once, bind off 3 stitches at the neck edge once, bind off 2 stitches at the neck edge once, then decrease 1 stitch at the neck edge every row twice—15 (17, 19, 21, 23, 25) stitches remain.

Continue even until the piece measures approximately 20½ (20½, 21, 21½, 22, 22)"/[52 (52, 53.5, 54.5, 56, 56)cm] from the beginning, ending after a wrong-side row.

SHAPE SHOULDERS
Bind off 5 (5, 6, 7, 8, 8) stitches at the armhole edge twice.

Work one row even.

Bind off 5 (7, 7, 7, 7, 9) stitches.

Place markers for 5 (5, 5, 5, 6, 6) buttons, making the first 1"/[2.5cm] from the lower edge, the last ½"/[1.5cm] from beginning of the lapel, with the others evenly spaced in between.

Right Front
With the smaller needles, cast on 41 (45, 49, 53, 57, 61) stitches.

Begin working seed stitch, and work even until the piece measures approximately 1"/[2.5cm] from the beginning, ending after a wrong-side row.

Change to the larger needles; make the first buttonhole as you work seed stitch across the first 7 stitches (see Notes), and work reverse stockinette stitch to the end of the row.

Continue even in the patterns as established until the piece measures approximately 2½"/[6.5cm] from the beginning, ending after a wrong-side row.

DECREASE FOR WAIST
Making buttonholes opposite the markers on the Left Front, work fully fashioned decreases (see Notes) at the armhole edge on the next row, then every 8 rows 3 times, *and at the same time,* when 38 (42, 46, 50, 54, 58) stitches remain and the piece measures

approximately 5½"/[14cm] from the beginning, place the pocket lining as follows on a right-side row: Work across the first 9 (11, 14, 16, 18, 20), stitches, slip the next 21 stitches onto a holder, purl across 21 stitches from pocket lining holder (with the purl side up), purl to the end of the row.

Once all waist decreases are completed, 37 (41, 45, 49, 53, 57) stitches remain.

Continue even until the piece measures approximately 8"/[20.5cm] from the beginning, ending after a wrong-side row.

INCREASE FOR BUST
Work fully fashioned increases (see Notes) at the armhole edge on the next row, then every other row 3 times—41 (45, 49, 53, 57, 61) stitches.

Continue even until the piece measures approximately 12½"/[32cm] from the beginning, ending after a right-side row.

SHAPE ARMHOLE
Bind off 4 (5, 6, 7, 8, 9) stitches at the armhole edge once, bind off 2 (3, 3, 4, 4, 5) stitches at the armhole edge once, work fully fashioned decreases (see Notes)

at the armhole edge every other row 1 (1, 2, 1, 4, 4) times, then every 4 rows 2 (2, 2, 3, 2, 2) times, *and at the same time,* when the piece measures approximately 13½ (13½, 14, 14½, 15, 15)"/[34.5 (34.5, 35.5, 37, 38, 38)cm] from the beginning, ending after a wrong-side row, place a marker between the seed stitch buttonband and the reverse stockinette stitches, and shape the lapel as follows:

SHAPE LAPEL

LAPEL INCREASE ROW (RS): Work in seed stitch to the marker, M1 knitwise or purlwise as needed to maintain the seed stitch pattern, slip the marker, work to the end of the row. Repeat the Lapel Increase Row every 10 rows 3 more times, working new stitches in seed stitch as they accumulate—36 (38, 40, 42, 43, 45) stitches.

Remove the marker, and continue even until the piece measures approximately 18½ (18½, 19, 19½, 20, 20)"/[47 (47, 48.5, 49.5, 51, 51)cm] from the beginning, ending after a wrong-side row.

SHAPE NECK

Bind off 8 (8, 8, 8, 7, 7) stitches at the beginning of the next row, then bind off 6 stitches at the neck edge once, bind off 3 stitches at the neck edge once, bind off 2 stitches at the neck edge once, then decrease 1 stitch at the neck edge every row twice—15 (17, 19, 21, 23, 25) stitches remain.

Continue even until the piece measures approximately 20½ (20½, 21, 21½, 22, 22)"/[52 (52, 53.5, 54.5, 56, 56)cm] from the beginning, ending after a right-side row.

SHAPE SHOULDERS

Bind off 5 (5, 6, 7, 8, 8) stitches at the armhole edge twice.

Work one row even.

Bind off 5 (7, 7, 7, 7, 9) stitches.

Sleeves *(Make 2)*

FIRST PIECE OF CUFF

With the smaller needles, cast on 19 stitches.

Begin working seed stitch, and work even until the piece measures approximately 2½"/[6.5cm] from the beginning, ending after a wrong-side row, and on the

last row, use the M1 increase (page 14) to increase 1 stitch at the beginning of the row—20 stitches.

Slip the stitches onto a holder.

SECOND PIECE OF CUFF

Work as for the first piece, but on the last row, use the M1 increase to increase 1 stitch at the end of the row—20 stitches.

JOIN CUFF

With the right sides facing and the larger needles, purl across 20 stitches from the first side of the cuff, then purl across 20 stitches from the second piece of cuff—40 stitches.

Continue working reverse stockinette stitch, and work fully fashioned increases (see Notes) each side every other row 0 (0, 0, 0, 2, 2) times, every 4 rows 0 (0, 5, 11, 13, 13) times, every 6 rows 0 (8, 6, 2, 0, 0) times, then every 8 rows 7 (1, 0, 0, 0, 0) times—54 (58, 62, 66, 70, 70) stitches.

Continue even until the piece measures approximately 12½"/[32cm] from the beginning, or to the desired length to the underarm, ending after a wrong-side row.

SHAPE CAP

Bind off 4 (5, 6, 7, 8, 9) stitches at the beginning of the next 2 rows, then work fully fashioned decreases (see Notes) each side every 4 rows 0 (0, 0, 0, 0, 1) time, every other row 11 (10, 12, 13, 16, 14) times, then every row 1 (3, 2, 2, 0, 0) times—22 stitches remain.

Bind off 2 stitches at the beginning of the next 4 rows—14 stitches remain.

Bind off.

Finishing

Darn in all remaining yarn tails (page 156).

Block all pieces to the finished measurements (page 156).

COLLAR

With the smaller needles, cast on 73 stitches.

Begin seed stitch, and work even until the piece measures approximately 2"/[5cm] from the beginning.

Decrease 1 stitch each side every row 10 times—53 stitches remain.

Bind off in the pattern.

Sew shoulder seams.

With the right side of the collar facing to the right side, sew the bound-off stitches of the collar to the neckline, leaving approximately 2"/[5cm] unsewn.

Set in the sleeves.

Sew the side and sleeve seams.

POCKET EDGINGS

With the right side facing and using the smaller needles, pick up and knit 21 stitches from one pocket holder.

Begin seed stitch, and work even until the edging measures approximately 1"/[2.5cm].

Bind off in pattern.

Repeat for the other pocket holder.

Sew pocket linings to the wrong side of Fronts. Sew sides of pocket edgings to the right side of Fronts.

Sew on the buttons where marked.

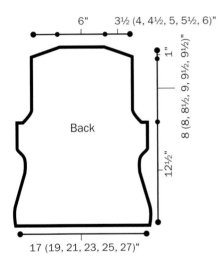

Back

6"

3½ (4, 4½, 5, 5½, 6)"

1"

8 (8, 8½, 9, 9½, 9½)"

12½"

17 (19, 21, 23, 25, 27)"

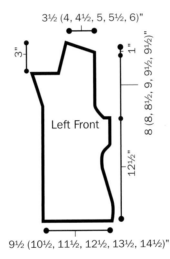

Left Front

3½ (4, 4½, 5, 5½, 6)"

3"

1"

8 (8, 8½, 9, 9½, 9½)"

12½"

9½ (10½, 11½, 12½, 13½, 14½)"

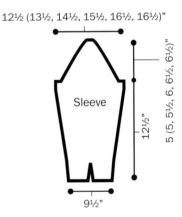

Sleeve

12½ (13½, 14½, 15½, 16½, 16½)"

5 (5, 5½, 6, 6½, 6½)"

12½"

9½"

Ooh-La-La Skirt

Worked almost entirely in the round, this flirty fit 'n' flare skirt is easy to knit and fun to wear. Careful placement of stitch markers means you won't have to count every stitch as you go. Since this design is worked in the round, only simple knit decreases are used for shaping. Go for it!

Skill Level
Advanced beginner

Sizes
Extra Small (Small, Medium, Large, 1X, 2X, 3X). Instructions are for the smallest size, with changes for other sizes noted in parentheses as necessary.

Finished Measurements
Waist (*before elastic*): 28 (30½, 34, 38, 42, 46, 49)"/[71 (77.5, 86, 96.5, 106.5, 117, 124.5)cm]
Hip: 33¾ (37½, 41, 44½, 48, 55, 58½)"/[85.5 (95.5, 104, 113, 122, 139.5, 149)cm]
Length: 24"/[61cm]

Materials
- JCA/Artful Yarns' *Lustro* (4-medium/worsted weight; 36% viscose/25% acrylic/20% mohair/19% nylon; each approximately 1¾ oz/[50g] and 148 yds/[135.5m]): 5 (5, 6, 7, 8, 9, 10) balls of Emerald #3903 Medium
- Size 8 (5mm) 36"/[90cm] circular knitting needle or size needed to obtain gauge
- Size 6 (4mm) 36"/[90cm] circular knitting needle
- 17 stitch markers (1 in a contrasting color for the beginning of rounds)
- Elastic, ¾"/[2cm] wide, cut to fit waist
- Zipper, 6"/[15cm]
- Blunt-end yarn needle
- Pins
- Thread in contrast color for basting zipper
- Sharp sewing needle
- Thread to match the yarn color

Gauge
18 stitches and 26 rounds = 4"/[10cm] in stockinette stitch with the larger needle.
To save time, take time to check gauge.

Fit
Close-fitting

Figure Flattery

Think you can't wear a knit skirt? Nonsense! Fun flounces add movement and grace to this design, and a smooth waistband makes it sleek. It's easy to adjust the length of the elastic for a flattering custom fit. Subtle vertical lines magically elongate the body.

Stitch Pattern

Stockinette Stitch Worked in the Round (*any number of stitches*)

ROUND 1 (RS): Knit around.

PATTERN ROUND: As Round 1.

Special Abbreviation

S2kp2 = Centered double decrease = Slip the next 2 stitches as if to k2tog, k1, pass the 2 slipped stitches over the knit stitch.

Notes

- This skirt is made in the round in one piece from the bottom up.
- Use a different colored marker for the beginning of the round.
- To work the pattern as established, knit the knit stitches and purl the purl stitches as you see them.
- The knit waist circumference has approximately 4"/ [10cm] of ease and will be gathered in by the elastic for a perfect fit.

Skirt

With the larger needle, *loosely* cast on 408 (408, 424, 440, 456, 488, 520) stitches.

Place a marker to indicate the beginning of the round; join, being careful not to twist the stitches.

ROUND 1 (RS): K11 (11, 12, 13, 14, 16, 18), *p29, k22 (22, 24, 26, 28, 32, 36); repeat from the * around, ending the round with p29, k11 (11, 12, 13, 14, 16, 18).

Work 1 round in the established pattern.

DECREASE ROUND 1: K10 (10, 11, 12, 13, 15, 17), *place a marker, ssk, p27, k2tog, place a marker, k20 (20, 22, 24, 26, 30, 34) stitches; repeat from the * around, ending the round with place a marker, ssk, p27, k2tog, place a marker, k10 (10, 11, 12, 13, 15, 17)— 392 (392, 408, 424, 440, 472, 504) stitches remain.

Work 1 round even.

DECREASE ROUND 2: Knit to the first marker, *slip the marker, ssk, purl to 2 stitches before the next marker, k2tog, slip the marker, knit to the next marker; repeat from the * around—376 (376, 392, 408, 424, 456, 488) stitches remain.

Repeat the last 2 rounds 11 more times—200 (200, 216, 232, 248, 280, 312) stitches remain.

Work 1 round even.

DECREASE ROUND 3: Knit to the first marker, *slip the marker, ssk, k1, k2tog, slip the marker, knit to the next marker; repeat from the * around—184 (184, 200, 216, 232, 264, 296) stitches remain.

Knit 1 round.

DECREASE ROUND 4: Knit to the first marker, *slip the marker, s2kp2, slip the marker; knit to the next marker; repeat from the * around—168 (168, 184, 200, 216, 248, 280) stitches remain.

NEXT ROUND: Knit to the first marker, *slip the marker, slip 1 purlwise (page 152), slip the marker, knit to the next marker; repeat from the * around.

Knit 1 round.

Repeat the last 2 rounds until the piece measures approximately 9 (18, 18, 18, 18, 18, 9)"/[23 (45.5, 45.5, 45.5, 45.5, 45.5, 23)cm] from the beginning, ending after a plain knit round.

FOR SIZES EXTRA SMALL AND 3X ONLY

NEXT ROUND: Repositioning markers as necessary so that they are on either side of the decrease stitch, *knit to 1 stitch before the next slipped stitch, s2kp2; repeat from the * around—152 (__, __, __, __, __, 264) stitches remain.

NEXT ROUND: Knit to the first marker, *slip the marker, slip 1 purlwise, slip the marker, knit to the next marker; repeat from the * around.

Knit 1 round.

Repeat the last 2 rounds until the piece measures approximately 18 (__, __, __, __, __, 18)"/[45.5 (__, __, __, __, __, 45.5)cm] from the beginning, ending after a plain knit round.

FOR ALL SIZES

Remove all markers. Begin working stockinette stitch back and forth in rows, continuing to slip the slipped stitches on right-side rows and purling all stitches on wrong-side rows.

Work even until the piece measures approximately 19½"/[49.5cm] from the beginning.

NEXT ROW (RS): *Knit to 1 stitch before the next slipped stitch, s2kp2; repeat from the * to the end of the row—136 (152, 168, 184, 200, 232, 248) stitches remain.

Continuing to slip the slipped stitches on right-side rows, work even until the piece measures approximately 23"/[58.5cm] from the beginning, ending after completing a wrong-side row.

DECREASE FOR WAISTBAND

NEXT ROW (RS): Knit across, and use the k2tog method to decrease 10 (14, 15, 13, 11, 25, 28) stitches evenly across—126 (138, 153, 171, 189, 207, 220) stitches remain.

WAISTBAND

Change to the smaller needle, and work even until the waistband measures approximately 2"/[5cm].

Bind off *loosely*.

Finishing

Darn in all remaining yarn tails (page 156).

Block the piece to the finished measurements (page 156).

Fold the waistband in half to the wrong side, insert the elastic, and *loosely* whipstitch (page 157) into place.

Secure elastic, and sew the opening closed.

Sew in zipper at side seam (page 157).

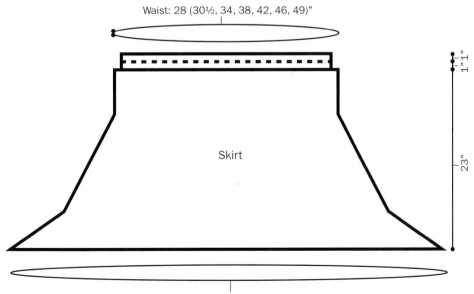

Waist: 28 (30½, 34, 38, 42, 46, 49)"

Skirt

1" 1"

23"

Lower Edge (plus flounces): 91 (91, 94, 98, 101½, 108½, 115½)"

Aberdeen

Practice stranded colorwork technique as you knit this showstopper. It is worked entirely in the round with steeks at the neckline and sleeve caps, with single purl stitches at the sides to give the appearance of seams.

Skill Level
Experienced

Sizes
Small (Medium, Large, 1X, 2X, 3X). Instructions are for the smallest size, with changes for the other sizes noted in parentheses as necessary.

Finished Measurements
Bust: 34¼ (38, 41½, 46½, 50, 53½)"/[87 (96.5, 105.5, 118, 127, 136)cm]
Hip: 36 (39½, 43, 48¼, 53½, 55)"/[91 (100.5, 109, 122.5, 136, 139.5)cm]
Length (*hemmed*): 20½ (21¼, 21½, 22, 22½, 23½)"/[52 (54, 54.5, 56, 57, 59.5)cm]

Materials
• Simply Shetland/Jamieson's *Spindrift* (1-super fine/fingering weight; 100% wool; each approximately 1 oz/[25g] and 115 yds/[105m]): 3 (3, 4, 4, 5, 5) balls of Lupin #629 (A), 2 (3, 3, 4, 4, 5) balls *each* of #685 Delph (B), #676 Sapphire (C), #1010 Seabright (D), and #135 Surf (E), 3 (3, 3, 4, 4, 4) balls of #764 Cloud (F), 1 (1, 1, 1, 1, 2) balls of #350 Lemon (G), and 1 (2, 2, 2, 2, 3) balls of #365 Chartreuse (H)

  🧵**1** Super Fine
• Size 1 (2.25mm) 29"/[74cm] circular needle
• Size 1 (2.25mm) 24"/[60cm] circular needle
• Size 1 (2.25mm) double-pointed needles (set of 4)
• Size 3 (3.25mm) 29"/[74cm] circular needle, or size needed to obtain gauge
• Size 3 (3.25mm) 24"/[60cm] circular needle, or size needed to obtain gauge
• Size 3 (3.25mm) 16"/[40cm] circular needle, or size needed to obtain gauge
• Size 3 (3.25mm) double-pointed needles (set of 4)
• 8 stitch markers (1 in a different color from the others to mark the beginning of rounds)
• Blunt-end yarn needle
• Size B/1 (2.25mm) crochet hook for crocheted steek (optional)

Gauge
28 stitches and 32 rounds = 4"/[10cm] in stranded 2-color stockinette stitch with the larger needle. *To save time, take time to check gauge.*

Stitch Patterns
Lower Hem Pattern (*multiple of 12 stitches*)
See chart.

Peaked Fair Isle Pattern (*multiple of 12 stitches*)
See chart.

Notes

- This sweater is worked entirely in the round from the bottom up, using steeks (page 153) for the armhole and neck shapings; the sleeves are worked in the round separately from the body, using a steek to shape the sleeve cap.
- The 9-stitch steeks are worked in a vertical stripe pattern as follows: *k1 with the background color of the round, k1 with the pattern color of the round; repeat from * 3 times, k1 with the background color. On color-change rounds, change colors in the middle of the first steek.
- The steek stitches are not included in the stitch counts; it is the knitter's choice if she wants to use a different-sized steek.
- When casting on for the steeks, use the e-wrap cast-on (page 150), alternating colors to match the steek stripe pattern.
- To increase within the pattern, use the lifted increase technique (page 14) in the color needed to maintain the pattern.
- The sweater is designed so that the patterns on the body and sleeves will line up at the armhole.
- For sweater assembly, refer to the illustration for set-in construction on page 158.

Body

With the smaller circular needle and A, use the provisional cast-on (page 151) to cast on 256 (280, 304, 340, 376, 388) stitches. Place a marker for the beginning of the round and join, being careful not to twist the stitches.

HEM

Beginning the Lower Hem Pattern where marked for your desired size, *work Round 1 of the pattern across the first 127 (139, 151, 169, 187, 193) stitches, place a marker, p1 in the background color for the "seam stitch," place a marker; repeat from the * once more.

Continue in the pattern, purling the "seam stitches" in the background color, until Round 12 is completed.

TURNING ROUND FOR HEM: Change to the larger needle; continuing with A and slipping markers, * slip 1 with the yarn in front, p1; repeat from the * around.

SET UP MAIN PATTERN

Beginning the Peaked Fair Isle Pattern where marked for your desired size and slipping markers, *work Round 1 of the pattern to the marker, p1 in the background color; repeat from the * once more.

Continue in the pattern, purling the "seam stitches" in the background color, until the Peaked Fair Isle Pattern section measures the same as the length of the hem to the Turning Round.

FOLD UP HEM

Carefully remove the crocheted chain from the provisional cast-on, and transfer the stitches onto the smaller needle as they are released from the chain. Fold the hem in half with the knit side on the outside, and hold the smaller needle behind the main knitting needle. With both needles in your left hand, continue the Peaked Fair Isle Pattern and k2tog (1 stitch from

the main needle and 1 stitch from the smaller needle) all the way around to close the hem.

Work 1 round in the pattern.

SHAPE WAIST

NEXT (DECREASE) ROUND: *K2tog, knit to 2 stitches before the first marker, ssk, slip the marker, p1, slip the marker; repeat from the * once—252 (276, 300, 336, 372, 384) stitches remain.

Repeat the Decrease Round every other round 2 (7, 7, 8, 12, 7) more times, then every 4 rounds 8 (6, 6, 6, 4, 7) times—212 (224, 248, 280, 308, 328) stitches remain.

Work even until the piece measures approximately 6½ (6¾, 7, 7, 7¼, 7¾)"/[16.5 (17, 18, 18, 18.5, 19.5) cm] from the beginning.

NEXT (INCREASE) ROUND: *Work a right lifted increase (page 15), knit to the marker, work a left lifted increase (page 14), slip the marker, p1, slip the marker; repeat from the * once—216 (228, 252, 284, 312, 332) stitches.

Repeat the Increase Round every 4 rounds 7 (5, 4, 5, 5, 4) more times, then every other round 0 (5, 6, 6, 5, 7) times—244 (268, 292, 328, 352, 376) stitches, with 122 (134, 146, 164, 176, 188) stitches each, Front and Back.

Work even until the piece measures approximately 13 (13½, 13½, 14, 14, 14½)"/[33 (34.5, 34.5, 35.5, 35.5, 37)cm] from the beginning, ending 10 (13, 14, 17, 21, 25) stitches before the end of the round. Break the pattern color. *Make a note of which pattern round you end with.*

ESTABLISH ARMHOLE STEEKS AND SHAPE ARMHOLES

NEXT ROUND: Removing markers as you come to them, bind off 19 (25, 27, 33, 41, 49) stitches with the background color; rejoin the pattern color and work to 9 (12, 13, 16, 20, 24) stitches before the next marker, break the pattern color, bind off 19 (25, 27, 33, 41, 49) stitches with the background color, rejoin the pattern color, work to the end of the round—103 (109, 119, 131, 135, 139) stitches remain for both the Front and the Back.

NEXT ROUND: Alternating colors (see Notes), cast on 4 stitches for the armhole steek, place a marker for the beginning of the round, cast on 5 more stitches for the armhole steek, place a marker, work to the 2nd set of bound-off stitches, place a marker, cast on 9 stitches for the armhole steek, place a marker, work to the end of the round.

NEXT (DECREASE) ROUND: *Work the steek stitches, slip the marker, k2tog, work to 2 stitches before the next marker, ssk, slip the marker; repeat from the * once, then work the 4 remaining steek stitches—101 (107, 117, 129, 133, 137) stitches remain for both the Front and the Back.

Repeat the Decrease Round every other round 2 (2, 8, 12, 11, 10) times, then every 4 rounds 3 (3, 1, 0, 0, 0) times—91 (97, 99, 105, 111, 117) stitches remain for the Back when the armhole decreases are complete. *At the same time,* when the armholes measure ½ (¾, 1, 1, 1½, 2)"/[1.5 (2, 2.5, 2.5, 4, 5)cm], place markers on either side of the 19 center front stitches.

ESTABLISH FRONT NECK STEEK AND SHAPE FRONT NECK

NEXT ROUND: Work to the marked center front stitches and break the pattern color; using the background color and removing the markers, bind off 19 stitches for the front neck; rejoin the pattern color and work to the end of the round.

NEXT ROUND: Work around and cast on 9 stitches for the front neck steek over the bound-off stitches, placing a marker before and after the new set of cast-on stitches.

NEXT (NECK DECREASE) ROUND: Slipping markers as you come to them, work to 2 stitches before the front neck steek, ssk, work the front neck steek, k2tog, work to the end of the round.

Repeat the Neck Decrease Round every round 5 more times, every other round 6 times, then every 4 rounds twice—22 (25, 26, 29, 32, 35) Front stitches remain each side of the front neck steek.

Work even until the armholes measure approximately 6 (6¼, 6½, 6½, 7, 7½)"/[15 (16, 16.5, 16.5, 18, 19)cm].

ESTABLISH BACK NECK STEEK AND SHAPE BACK NECK

NEXT ROUND: Slipping the markers as you come to them, work to 24 (27, 28, 31, 34, 37) stitches past the second armhole steek and break the pattern

color; using the background color, bind off the next 43 stitches for the back neck; rejoin the pattern color and work to the end of the round.

NEXT ROUND: Work around and cast on 9 stitches over the bound-off stitches for the back neck steek, placing a marker before and after the new set of cast-on stitches.

NEXT (NECK DECREASE) ROUND: Slipping markers as you come to them, work to 2 stitches before the first back neck steek marker, ssk, work the back neck steek, k2tog, work to the end of the round—23 (26, 27, 30, 33, 36) Back stitches remain each side of the back neck steek.

Repeat the Neck Decrease Round once more—22 (25, 26, 29, 32, 35) Back stitches remain each side.

Work even until the armholes measure approximately 7½ (7¾, 8, 8, 8½, 9)"/[19 (19.5, 20.5, 20.5, 21.5, 23)cm].

With the background color, bind off all stitches.

Sleeves (Make 2)

With the smaller double-pointed needles and A, using the provisional cast-on technique (page 151), cast on 67 (67, 79, 79, 91, 91) stitches; place a marker for the beginning of the round and join, being careful not to twist the stitches.

HEM

Beginning the Lower Hem Pattern where marked for your desired size, work Round 1 of the pattern to the last stitch, place a marker, p1 in the background color for the "seam stitch."

Continue working the pattern, purling the "seam stitches" in the background color, until Round 12 is completed.

TURNING ROUND FOR HEM: Change to the larger double-pointed needles; continuing with A, *slip the next stitch with the yarn in front, p1; repeat from the * around.

SET UP MAIN PATTERN

Beginning the Peaked Fair Isle Pattern where marked for the sleeves, work Round 1 of the pattern to marker, slip the marker, p1 for the "seam stitch" in the background color.

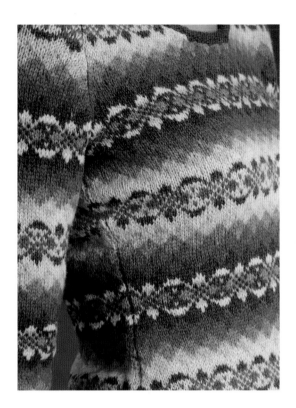

Continue in the pattern, purling the "seam stitches" in the background color, until the Peaked Fair Isle Pattern section measures the same as the length of the hem to the Turning Round.

FOLD UP HEM

Carefully remove the crocheted chain from the provisional cast-on, and transfer the stitches onto the smaller double-pointed needles as they are released from the chain. Fold the hem in half with the knit side on the outside, and hold the smaller needles behind the main needles. Holding smaller and larger needles in your left hand, continue the Peaked Fair Isle Pattern and k2tog (1 stitch from the main needle and 1 stitch from the smaller needle) all the way around to close the hem.

NEXT (INCREASE) ROUND: Work a right lifted increase, then continue in pattern to the marker, make a left lifted increase, slip the marker, p1 for the "seam stitch" in the background color—69 (69, 81, 81, 93, 93) stitches.

Repeat the Increase Round every 8 rounds 0 (5, 0, 0, 0, 1) times, every 10 rounds 5 (4, 0, 7, 0, 8) times, every 12 rounds 2 (0, 0, 1, 2, 0) times, every

14 rounds 0 (0, 4, 0, 4, 0) times, every 16 rounds 0 (0, 1, 0, 0, 0) times, changing to a circular needle as the stitches accumulate—83 (87, 91, 97, 105, 111) stitches.

Work even until the piece measures approximately 13 (13½, 13½, 14, 14, 14½)"/[33 (34.5, 34.5, 35.5, 35.5, 37) cm], ending 10 (13, 14, 17, 21, 25) stitches before the end of the round, ending after the same pattern round as the body up to the armhole.

ESTABLISH SLEEVE CAP STEEKS AND SHAPE CAP

NEXT ROUND: Break the pattern color; with the background color, bind off 19 (25, 27, 33, 41, 49) stitches; rejoin the pattern color and work to the end of the round—64 (62, 64, 64, 64, 62) stitches remain.

NEXT ROUND: Cast on 4 stitches for the sleeve cap steek, place a marker for the beginning of the round, cast on 5 more sleeve cap steek stitches, place a marker, work to the end of the round.

NEXT (SLEEVE CAP DECREASE) ROUND: Slipping the markers as you come to them, work 5 steek stitches, k2tog, work to the last 2 sleeve stitches, ssk, work the 4 remaining steek stitches—62 (60, 62, 62, 62, 60) sleeve stitches remain.

Repeat the Sleeve Cap Decrease Round every 4 rounds 0 (1, 2, 2, 5, 9) times, every other round 18 (18, 18, 18, 14, 8) times, then every round 2 (0, 0, 0, 0, 0) times,

changing to double-pointed needles as necessary—22 (22, 22, 22, 24, 26) sleeve stitches remain.

With the background color, bind off.

Finishing

Secure Front neck, Back neck, and armhole steeks (page 153).

Cut the steeks (page 154).

Block the pieces to the finished measurements (page 156).

Use mattress stitch (page 156) to sew the shoulder seams.

NECKBAND

With the right side facing, larger 16"/[40cm] circular needle, and 2 strands of A held together, pick up and knit 116 stitches around the neckline.

Purl 5 rounds.

Bind off purlwise, allowing the neckband to roll to the wrong side.

Set in the sleeves.

Trim the steeks as necessary; fold back and tack to wrong side.

NOTE

Measurements in the schematic illustrations are finished measurements, not including steek stitches.

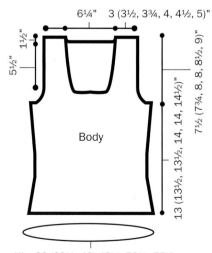

Body

6¼" 3 (3½, 3¾, 4, 4½, 5)"

1½"

5½"

7½ (7¾, 8, 8, 8½, 9)"

13 (13½, 13½, 14, 14, 14½)"

Hip: 36 (39½, 43, 48¼, 53½, 55)"
Bust: 34¼ (38, 41½, 46½, 50, 53½)"

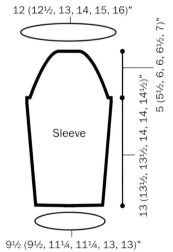

Sleeve

12 (12½, 13, 14, 15, 16)"

5 (5½, 6, 6, 6½, 7)"

13 (13½, 13½, 14, 14, 14½)"

9½ (9½, 11¼, 11¼, 13, 13)"

PEAKED FAIR ISLE PATTERN

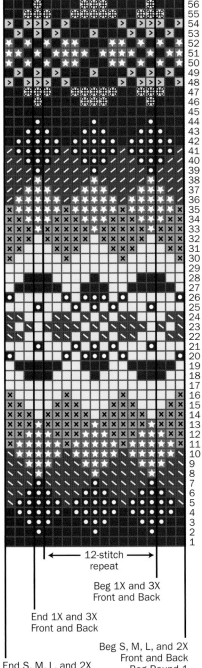

Color Key

■ = A

◉ = B

◣ = C

★ = D

☒ = E

□ = F

▦ = G

▷ = H

Stitch Key

□ = K

LOWER HEM FAIR ISLE PATTERN

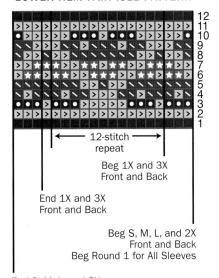

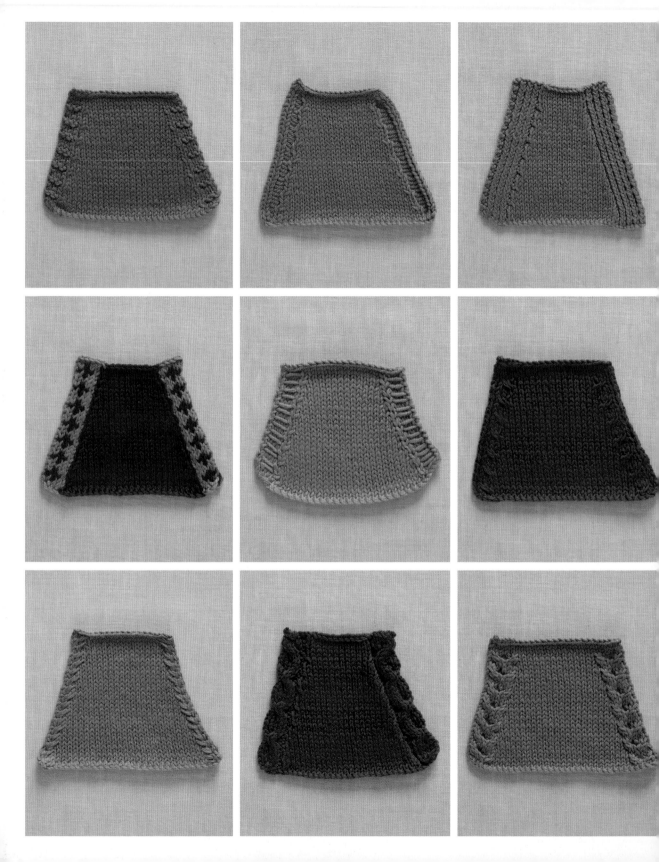

3

Designer
Details

Now that we've seen how easy it is to add fully fashioned shaping to any pattern, let's take a look at ways to use these elements to create knockout knits.

Designer Workshop

Enrich Your Knits!

If you'd like to add a special detail to your knitting, include some of the following decorative applications of fully fashioned shaping. They're great along raglan and other armhole shaping, as well as on either side of sleeve caps—even waist shaping! As a bonus, some of these design elements are noncurling, so they're ideal for incorporated neckbands and armhole bands, as in The Weekender (page 75). That way, you don't have to go back and pick up stitches later to finish the sweater. Hoorah!

The examples all use decreases, but increases could easily be used as well. Just substitute one of the increase methods (pages 14–16) inside the ornamental edges.

Garter Ridges

Here's an easy way to accentuate the shaped areas of a design with a bit of texture. Horizontal ridges of garter stitch are worked on 3 stitches just outside of the decreases as seen in the swatch below.

Swatch It Up

Give it a try! Knit up a sample with garter ridges defining the fully fashioned shaping. Just a little bit of texture can go a long way! Note that each 4-row repeat decreases 1 stitch on each side.

To begin, cast on 35 stitches.

Row 1 (RS): Knit.

Row 2: K3, purl to the last 3 stitches, k3.

Row 3: K3, ssk, knit to the last 5 stitches, k2tog, k3.

Row 4: As Row 2.

Repeat Rows 1–4 until 21 stitches remain.

Dropped Stitches

Knitters bend over backwards trying to prevent dropping their stitches, but this fully fashioned option allows you to intentionally drop them! It's a fun and novel way to draw attention to shaped areas. Prior to the shaping, one stitch is added by making a yarn over a few stitches in from the edge of the fabric; when all shaping is completed, the extra stitch is dropped from the needle and gently coaxed to "run" all the way

down. Take a look at the "deconstructed" results in the swatch above.

Swatch It Up

 Have a go at it: try a sample piece with intentionally dropped stitches. Note that each 4-row repeat decreases 1 stitch on each side.

To begin, cast on 35 stitches.

Set-Up Row (RS): K2, yarn over, knit to the last 2 stitches, yarn over, k2.

Row 1 (WS): Purl.

Row 2: Knit.

Row 3: As Row 1.

Row 4: K3, ssk, knit to the last 5 stitches, k2tog, k3.

Repeat Rows 1–4 until 21 stitches remain. ending after a wrong-side row.

Final Row (RS): K2, remove the next stitch from the left-hand needle and unravel it down to the original yarn over in the Set-up Row, knit to the last 3 stitches, remove the next stitch from the left-hand needle and unravel it down to the original yarn over, k2.

Doing the Twist

Here's a way to add lots of vertical lines to your knitting, each of them drawing the eye upward to create a flattering effect as seen in the swatch above. And it's so easy: just work a handful of stitches in a twisted rib pattern, knitting (page 150) or purling (page 152) *in the back loops* as you go. Fully fashioned decreases are worked in purl valleys so they are inconspicuous.

Swatch It Up

 Try it: Here's a sample swatch with fully fashioned decreases worked just inside twisted rib panels. Note that each 4-row repeat decreases one stitch on each side.

To begin, cast on 35 stitches.

Row 1 (RS): [K1 *through the back loop*, p1] 4 times, knit to the last 8 stitches, [p1, k1 *through the back loop*] 4 times.

Row 2: [P1 *through the back loop*, k1] 4 times, purl to the last 8 stitches, [k1, p1 *through the back loop*] 4 times.

Row 3 (Decrease Row): Work the first 7 stitches in the established pattern, p2tog, knit to the last 9 stitches, p2tog, work in pattern to the end of the row.

Row 4: As Row 2.

Repeat Rows 1–4 until 21 stitches remain.

Multicolor Bands

It's fun to incorporate color into knits, and here's a novel approach: Work narrow Fair Isle bands just outside the fully fashioned shaping as seen in the swatch above.

Swatch It Up

 Give it a spin! Knit a sample piece with Fair Isle bands accentuating the fully fashioned shaping. Of course, any Fair Isle chart can be used; the pattern in this example is 5 stitches wide. It's best to use opposite colors for the background in the solid sections and in the charted areas to provide high contrast. Note that each 4-row repeat decreases one stitch on each side.

To begin, cast on 35 stitches with the main color.

Row 1 (RS): Knit 5 stitches in the Fair Isle Pattern; with the main background color, knit to the last 5 stitches; knit 5 stitches in the Fair Isle Pattern.

Row 2: Purl 5 stitches in the Fair Isle Pattern; with the main background color, purl to the last 5 stitches; purl 5 stitches in the Fair Isle Pattern.

FAIR ISLE PATTERN
(over 5 stitches)

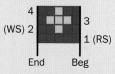

Color Key
■ = Contrast Color
□ = Background Color

Stitch Key
□ = K on RS; p on WS

Row 3 (Decrease Row): Knit 5 stitches in the Fair Isle Pattern; with the main background color, ssk, knit to the last 7 stitches, k2tog; knit 5 stitches in the Fair Isle Pattern.

Row 4: As Row 2.

Repeat Rows 1–4 until 21 stitches remain.

Horizontal Barred Stitches

For a bold fully fashioned effect, use slip stitch technique to create horizontal "floats" on the right side of the fabric as seen in the swatch above. Just be sure the working yarn is brought toward the knit side before slipping the stitches, and remember to return it to the back after slipping.

Swatch It Up

 You'll be surprised at how easy it is to achieve this effect. Give it a try! Note that each 4-row repeat decreases one stitch on each side.

To begin, cast on 35 stitches.

Row 1 (RS): K1, slip the next 3 stitches purlwise with the yarn in front, knit to the last 4 sts, slip the next 3 stitches purlwise with the yarn in front, k1.

Row 2: Purl.

Row 3 (Decrease Row): K1, slip the next 3 stitches purlwise with the yarn in front, ssk, knit to the last 6 stitches, k2tog, slip the next 3 stitches purlwise with the yarn in front, k1.

Row 4: As Row 2.

Repeat Rows 1–4 until 21 stitches remain.

Simple Cables

Sometimes little cables along shaped areas are all a design needs to stand out. Look at the swatch above. In that swatch, fully fashioned decreases are worked *within cables* on each side of the fabric. Wow!

Swatch It Up

Have a go at it: Try a swatch with cables along the fully fashioned shaping. In this example, each cable twists toward the selvedges. Note that each 4-row repeat decreases one stitch on each side.

To begin, cast on 35 stitches.

Row 1 (RS): Knit.

Row 2: Purl.

Row 3 (Decrease Row): K2, slip the next 2 stitches to a cable needle and hold in back, k1, ssk the stitches on the cable needle to combine them, knit to the last 5 stitches, slip the next stitch to a cable needle and hold in front, k2tog, k1 from the cable needle, k2.

Row 4: Purl.

Repeat Rows 1–4 until 21 stitches remain.

Raised Cables

For more stitch definition as seen in the swatch above, try this version of fully fashioned cabling.

Swatch It Up

Here's how to work fully fashioned shaping with pronounced cabled stitches twisting toward the interior of the fabric. This method would be quite flattering for raglan decreases, since all design elements would be pointing toward the neckline. Note that each 4-row repeat decreases one stitch on each side.

To begin, cast on 35 stitches.

Row 1 (RS): K1, slip the next stitch to a cable needle and hold in front, k2, k1 from the cable needle, knit to the last 4 stitches, slip the next 2 stitches to a cable needle and hold in back, k1, k2 from the cable needle, k1.

Row 2: Purl.

Row 3 (Decrease Row): K1, slip the next stitch to a cable needle and hold in front, ssk to combine the next 2 stitches on the left-hand needle, k1 from the cable needle, knit to the last 4 stitches, slip the next 2 stitches to a cable needle and hold in back, k1, k2tog the 2 stitches on the cable needle to combine them, k1.

Row 4: As Row 2.

Repeat Rows 1–4 until 21 stitches remain.

Exaggerated Cables

We can cross elongated stitches to create even more definition during fully fashioned shaping. In this case, one intentionally loose stitch on each side edge of the fabric is slipped for a few rows before cabling it. As seen in the swatch above, the twists slant toward the interior of the fabric and are loose, looking almost like hand embroidery. Try this technique on your next raglan sweater or sleeve cap.

Swatch It Up

Practice knitting fully fashioned decreases with elongated cable stitches as seen above. You'll need two safety pins to hold the slipped stitches. To work the elongated stitches on Row 1, first insert the right-hand needle purlwise (page 152) into the stitch on the left-hand needle, then wrap the yarn around the right-hand needle three times as you purl the stitch. It's easy! Note that each 4-row repeat decreases one stitch on each side.

To begin, cast on 35 stitches.

Row 1 (WS): P1, purl the next stitch *wrapping the yarn 3 times around the needle as you make the stitch,* purl to the last 2 stitches, purl the next stitch *wrapping the yarn 3 times around the needle as you make the stitch,* p1.

Row 2: K1, slip the next stitch onto a safety pin and allow it to hang to the front, knit to the last 2 stitches, slip the next stitch onto a safety pin and allow it to hang to the front, k1.

Row 3: Purl across, leaving the stitches on the safety pins hanging and unworked.

Row 4 (Decrease Row): K4, transfer the stitch from the safety pin to the left-hand needle, ssk, knit to the last 6 stitches (including the stitch on the safety pin), slip the next stitch to the right-hand needle, transfer the stitch from the safety pin to the left-hand needle, then slip the first stitch on the right-hand needle back onto the left-hand needle, k2tog, k4.

Repeat Rows 1–4 until 21 stitches remain.

Cables and Eyelets

For a beautiful effect on women's and kids' knits, incorporate this fully fashioned detail. It combines cable twists with lace, as seen in the swatch above.

Swatch It Up

Give this interesting fully fashioned technique a whirl. It uses both cables and eyelets to attract attention to the shaped area. Note that each 4-row repeat decreases one stitch on each side.

To begin, cast on 35 stitches.

Row 1 (RS): Knit.

Row 2: Purl.

Row 3 (Decrease Row): K1, slip the next stitch to a cable needle and hold in back, k2tog, k1

from the cable needle, yarn over, slip the next 2 stitches to a cable needle and hold in front, k1, ssk to combine the 2 stitches on the cable needle, knit to the last 7 stitches, slip the next stitch to a cable needle and hold in back, k2tog, k1 from the cable needle, yarn over, slip the next 2 stitches to a cable needle and hold in front, k1, ssk to combine the 2 stitches on the cable needle, k1.

Row 4: As Row 2.

Repeat Rows 1–4 until 21 stitches remain.

Honeycomb Cables

Here's a lovely way to highlight fully fashioned shaping! Half of a honeycomb cable is worked on each side of the fabric (just outside the shaping) as seen in the swatch above. Once the seams are sewn, the two halves meet to create a beautiful honeycomb cable (see swatch, above right). I used this designer detail in a raglan sweater in my book entitled *Cables Untangled* (Potter Craft, 2006).

Swatch It Up

Swatch a bit of fully fashioned shaping using honeycomb cables. Here, the decreases occur in the purl "valleys" that frame the cabled sections. Note that each 8-row repeat decreases two stitches on each side.

To begin, cast on 35 stitches.

Row 1 (RS): K1, slip the next 2 stitches to a cable needle and hold in front, k2, k2 from the cable needle, p2, knit to the last 7 stitches, p2, slip the next 2 stitches to a cable needle and hold in back, k2, k2 from the cable needle, k1.

Row 2 and all even rows: Knit the knit stitches and purl the purl stitches as you see them.

Row 3 (Decrease Row): K5, p1, p2tog, knit to the last 8 stitches, ssp, p1, k5.

Row 5: K1, slip the next 2 stitches to a cable needle and hold in back, k2, k2 from the cable needle, p2, knit to the last 7 stitches, p2, slip the next 2 stitches to a cable needle and hold in front, k2, k2 from the cable needle, k1.

Row 7 (Decrease Row): As Row 3.

Repeat Rows 1–8 until 19 stitches remain.

It's fun to explore different ways to add visual interest to fully fashioned shaping. Practice with the swatches in this section and then incorporate these details into your knitting. Of course, you don't have to limit your use of fully fashioned techniques to shaping waistlines; you can use them to add beautiful designer touches, from integrated V-necklines to cabled raglan elements. You, too, can be a designer!

Orvieto

In this great topper, braided cables travel along the raglan seams. They extend all the way down the side seams, too, creating a beautiful—and slimming!—effect.

Skill Level
Intermediate

Sizes
Extra Small (Small, Medium, Large, 1X, 2X, 3X). Instructions are for the smallest size, with changes for other sizes noted in parentheses as necessary.

Finished Measurements
Bust (*buttoned*): 34 (37¼, 41, 42¼, 46, 48½, 51½)"/[86 (94.5, 104, 107.5, 117, 123, 131)cm]
Length: 19¾"/[50cm]

Materials
- Lion Brand Yarn's *Alpine Tweed* (5-bulky weight; 100% wool; each approximately 3 oz/[85g] and 93 yds/[85m]): 9 (10, 11, 12, 13, 14, 15) balls of Chili #115  Bulky
- Size 10 (6mm) knitting needles or size needed to obtain gauge
- Size 10½ (6.5mm) knitting needles
- Cable needle
- 2 buttons, 1⅝"/[41mm] (JHB International's *Arles Style #51105* were used on sample garment)
- Blunt-end yarn needle
- Pointed sewing needle

Gauge
13 stitches and 22 rows = 4"/[10cm] in the Box Stitch Pattern with the smaller needles.
The 9-stitch Cable Panels each measure 1¾"/[4.5cm] across with the smaller needles.
To save time, take time to check gauge.

Stitch Patterns
Box Stitch Pattern (*multiple of 4 + 2 stitches*)
ROW 1 (RS): K2, *p2, k2; repeat from the * across.
ROW 2: P2, *k2, p2; repeat from the * across.
ROW 3: As Row 2.
ROW 4: As Row 1.
Repeat Rows 1–4 for the pattern.

Right Cable Panel (*over 9 stitches*)
See chart.

Left Cable Panel (*over 9 stitches*)
See chart.

Notes
- The instructions include 1 selvedge stitch on each side; these stitches are not included in the finished measurements.
- For fully fashioned raglan decreases: On right-side rows, work 8 stitches in pattern, ssp, work in pattern to the last 10 stitches, p2tog, work 8 stitches in pattern; on wrong-side rows, work 8 stitches in pattern, k2tog, work in pattern to the last 10 stitches, ssk, work 8 stitches in pattern.
- For sweater assembly, refer to the illustration for raglan construction on page 158.

Back
With the smaller needles, cast on 64 (68, 72, 76, 80, 88, 92) stitches.

SET UP THE PATTERNS
Working Row 1 of each pattern, work the Right Cable Panel across 9 stitches; work the Box Stitch Pattern over 46 (50, 54, 58, 62, 70, 74) stitches; work the Left Cable Panel across 9 stitches.

Continue in the established patterns until the piece measures approximately 11 (10½, 10, 9½, 9, 8½, 8½)"/[28 (26.5, 25.5, 24, 23, 21.5, 21.5)cm] from the beginning, ending after a wrong-side row.

SHAPE RAGLAN
Work fully fashioned raglan decreases (see Notes) every row 0 (0, 0, 1, 2, 8, 12) times, every other row 17 (20, 22, 23, 24, 22, 20) times, then every 4 rows 1 (0, 0, 0, 0, 0, 0) time—28 stitches remain.

Work 1 (1, 0, 0, 0, 0, 0) row even.

Bind off in pattern, working k2tog over the sixth and seventh stitches of the Right Cable Pattern and ssk over the third and fourth stitches of the Left Cable Pattern to avoid cable splay.

Left Front
With the smaller needles, cast on 43 (43, 47, 47, 51, 55, 55) stitches.

SET UP THE PATTERNS
Working Row 1 of each pattern, work the Right Cable Panel across 9 stitches; work the Box Stitch Pattern to the end of the row.

Continue in the established patterns until the piece measures approximately 11 (10½, 10, 9½, 9, 8½, 8½)"/[28 (26.5, 25.5, 24, 23, 21.5, 21.5)cm] from the beginning, ending after a wrong-side row.

SHAPE RAGLAN AND NECK
Work fully fashioned raglan decreases at the armhole edge every row 0 (0, 0, 1, 2, 8, 12) times, every other row 17 (20, 22, 23, 24, 22, 20) times, then every 4 rows 1 (0, 0, 0, 0, 0, 0) time, *and at the same time,* when the piece measures approximately ½"/[1.5cm] less than the Back, ending after a right-side row, shape the neck as follows: Bind off 14 (12, 14, 12, 14, 14, 12) stitches at the neck edge once, then decrease 1 stitch at the neck edge twice.

Once all raglan decreases are completed, work 1 (1, 0, 0, 0, 0, 0) row even on remaining 9 stitches.

Bind off in pattern, working k2tog over the sixth and seventh stitches of the Right Cable Pattern and ssk over the third and fourth stitches of the Left Cable Pattern to avoid cable splay.

Right Front

With the smaller needles, cast on 43 (43, 47, 47, 51, 55, 55) stitches.

SET UP THE PATTERNS

Working Row 1 of each pattern, work the Box Stitch Pattern across 34 (34, 38, 38, 42, 46, 46) stitches; work the Left Cable Panel across 9 stitches.

Continue in the established patterns until the piece measures approximately 11 (10½, 10, 9½, 9, 8½, 8½)"/[28 (26.5, 25.5, 24, 23, 21.5, 21.5)cm] from the beginning, ending after a wrong-side row.

SHAPE RAGLAN AND NECK

Work fully fashioned raglan decreases at the armhole edge every row 0 (0, 0, 1, 2, 8, 12) times, every other row 17 (20, 22, 23, 24, 22, 20) times, then every 4 rows 1 (0, 0, 0, 0, 0, 0) time, *and at the same time,* when the piece measures approximately 16½"/[42cm] from the beginning, ending after a wrong-side row, make 2 buttonholes as follows: Work 4 stitches in pattern, bind off 2 stitches, work to the last 6 stitches, bind off 2 stitches, work to the end of the row. On the subsequent row, use the cable cast-on technique to cast on 2 stitches over the bound-off stitches of the previous row.

Complete same as the Left Front.

Sleeves *(Make 2)*

With the smaller needles, cast on 56 stitches.

SET UP THE PATTERNS

Working Row 1 of each pattern, work the Right Cable Panel across 9 stitches; work the Box Stitch Pattern across 38 stitches; work the Left Cable Panel across the last 9 stitches.

Continue in the established patterns until the piece measures approximately 11 (10½, 10, 9½, 9, 8½, 8½)"/[28 (26.5, 25.5, 24, 23, 21.5, 21.5)cm] from the beginning, ending after a wrong-side row.

SHAPE RAGLAN

Work fully fashioned raglan decreases each side every other row 17 (16, 14, 13, 11, 10, 10) times, then every 4 rows 1 (2, 4, 5, 7, 8, 8) times—20 stitches remain.

Work 1 (1, 0, 1, 0, 0, 0) row even.

Bind off in pattern, working k2tog over the sixth and seventh stitches of the Right Cable Pattern and ssk over the third and fourth stitches of the Left Cable Pattern to avoid cable splay.

Finishing

Darn in all remaining yarn tails (page 156).

Block all pieces to the finished measurements (page 156).

Sew the raglan seams.

COLLAR

With the wrong side facing and using the smaller needles, beginning and ending approximately 1¾"/[4.5cm] from the Front edge, pick up and knit 54 stitches along the neckline.

Beginning with Row 2 of the pattern, work the Box Stitch Pattern until the collar measures approximately 3½"/[9cm] from the beginning, and *at the same time,* on wrong-side rows, increase as follows, working new stitches into the established pattern: Work 2 stitches in pattern, M1 knitwise or purlwise (page 14), depending on what the next stitch in the pattern is, work to the last 2 stitches, M1 knitwise or purlwise (depending on what the next stitch in the pattern is), work 2 stitches in pattern.

Change to the larger needles, and continue increasing on wrong-side rows as before until the collar measures approximately 5½"/[14cm].

Bind off in pattern.

Sew the side and sleeve seams.

Sew on the buttons opposite the buttonholes.

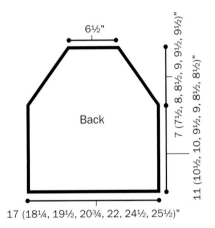

Back

6½"

7 (7½, 8, 8½, 9, 9½, 9½)"

11 (10½, 10, 9½, 9, 8½, 8½)"

17 (18¼, 19½, 20¾, 22, 24½, 25½)"

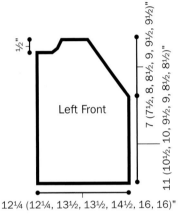

Left Front

½"

7 (7½, 8, 8½, 9, 9½, 9½)"

11 (10½, 10, 9½, 9, 8½, 8½)"

12¼ (12¼, 13½, 13½, 14½, 16, 16)"

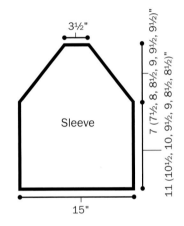

Sleeve

3½"

7 (7½, 8, 8½, 9, 9½, 9½)"

11 (10½, 10, 9½, 9, 8½, 8½)"

15"

LEFT CABLE PANEL

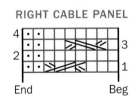

4
2
3
1
End   Beg

RIGHT CABLE PANEL

4
2
3
1
End   Beg

Stitch Key

☐ = K on RS; p on WS

• = P on RS; k on WS

= Slip 2 sts onto cn and hold in back; k2; k2 from cn

= Slip 2 sts onto cn and hold in front; k2; k2 from cn

Cables 'n' Ribs

This slightly fitted pullover will hug you in all the right places. Fully fashioned decreases at the raglan seams create a perfectly seamless look.

Skill Level
Intermediate

Sizes
Extra Small (Small, Medium, Large, 1X, 2X, 3X). Instructions are for the smallest size, with changes for other sizes noted in parentheses as necessary.

Finished Measurements
Bust: 32 (35, 39, 42, 45, 49, 52)"/[81 (89, 99, 106.5, 114, 124.5, 132) cm]
Length: 21½ (22¾, 23¾, 24¼, 24¾, 25½, 26½)"/[54.5 (58, 60.5, 61.5, 63, 65, 67.5)cm]

Materials
- Classic Elite Yarns' *Portland Tweed* (4-medium/worsted weight; 50% virgin wool/25% alpaca/25% viscose; each approximately 1¾ oz/[50g] and 120 yds/[132m]): 9 (10, 11, 12, 13, 14, 15) balls of Tidal Foam #5004 **4** Medium
- Size 5 (3.75mm) knitting needles
- Size 7 (4.5mm) knitting needles or size needed to obtain gauge
- Cable needle
- 2 stitch markers
- Blunt-end yarn needle

Gauge
24 stitches and 26 rows = 4"/[10cm] in the Rib Pattern, *unstretched*, with the larger needles.
30 stitches and 26 rows = 4"/[10cm] in the Cable Pattern with the larger needles.
To save time, take time to check gauge.

Stitch Patterns
Rib Pattern (*multiple of 5 + 2 stitches*)
ROW 1 (RS): K2, *p3, k2; repeat from the * across.
ROW 2: P2, *k3, p2; repeat from the * across.
Repeat Rows 1 and 2 for the pattern.

Cable Pattern (*multiple of 30 + 26 stitches*)
See chart.

Notes

- For a perfect close fit, this sweater is designed with negative ease. The ribbed pattern will allow the fabric to stretch to fit the body, so knit the size you would normally knit for yourself.
- For fully fashioned body decreases: Work 11 (16, 21, 26, 31, 36, 41) stitches in pattern, ssk, work in pattern to the last 13 (18, 23, 28, 33, 38, 43) stitches, k2tog, work in pattern to the end of the row.
- For fully fashioned body increases: Work 12 (17, 22, 27, 32, 37, 42) stitches in pattern, M1 purlwise (page 15), work in pattern to the last 12 (17, 22, 27, 32, 37, 42) stitches, M1 purlwise, work in pattern to the end of the row.
- For fully fashioned raglan decreases: For right-side rows, work 6 stitches in pattern, ssk, work in pattern to the last 8 stitches, k2tog, work in pattern to the end of the row; for wrong-side rows, work 6 stitches in pattern, p2tog, work in pattern to the last 8 stitches, ssp, work in pattern to the end of the row.
- For fully fashioned sleeve increases: Work 7 stitches in pattern, M1 knitwise (page 14) or purlwise, depending on what the new stitch will be when incorporated into the Rib Pattern, work in pattern to the last 7 stitches, M1 knitwise or purlwise, depending on what the new stitch will be when incorporated into the Rib Pattern, work in pattern to the end of the row.
- For sweater assembly, refer to the illustration for raglan construction on page 158.

Back

With the larger needles, cast on 110 (120, 130, 140, 150, 160, 170) stitches.

SET UP BORDER PATTERNS

ROW 1 (RS): Work Row 1 of the Rib Pattern over the first 12 (17, 22, 27, 32, 37, 42) stitches, [p4, k2, p3, k2] twice, p4, k4, [p4, k2, p3, k2] twice, p4, k4, [p4, k2, p3, k2] twice, p4, then work Row 1 of the Ribbed Pattern over 12 (17, 22, 27, 32, 37, 42) stitches to end the row.

ROW 2 (WS): Knit the knit stitches and purl the purl stitches.

ROW 3: Work 12 (17, 22, 27, 32, 37, 42) stitches in pattern, [p4, k2, p3, k2] twice, p4, slip 2 stitches to a cn and hold in back, k2, k2 from the cn, [p4, k2, p3,

k2] twice, p4, k4, [p4, k2, p3, k2] twice, p4, work 12 (17, 22, 27, 32, 37, 42) stitches in pattern.

ROW 4: Knit the knit stitches and purl the purl stitches.

ROWS 5 AND 6: Repeat Rows 1 and 2.

SET UP MAIN PATTERNS

ROW 7: Working Row 1 of each pattern, work 12 (17, 22, 27, 32, 37, 42) stitches in the Rib Pattern, place a marker, work the Cable Pattern over the next 86 stitches, place a marker, work 12 (17, 22, 27, 32, 37, 42) stitches in the Rib Pattern.

DECREASE FOR WAIST

Continue the established patterns, *and at the same time,* work fully fashioned body decreases (see Notes) every 10 rows 0 (0, 0, 0, 0, 2, 3) times, every 8 rows 3 (3, 3, 4, 4, 2, 1) times, then every 6 rows 1 (1, 1, 0, 0, 0, 0) time—102 (112, 122, 132, 142, 152, 162) stitches remain.

Continue even until the piece measures approximately 6½ (6½, 6¾, 7, 7, 7¼, 7½)"/[16.5 (16.5, 17, 18,

18, 18.5, 19)cm] from the beginning, ending after a wrong-side row.

INCREASE FOR BUST

Continue the established patterns, *and at the same time,* work fully fashioned body increases (see Notes) every 6 rows 1 (1, 1, 0, 0, 0, 0) time, every 8 rows 3 (3, 3, 4, 4, 2, 1) times, then every 10 rows 0 (0, 0, 0, 0, 2, 3) times, working the new stitches into the Rib Pattern—110 (120, 130, 140, 150, 160, 170) stitches.

Continue even until the piece measures approximately 13 (13¾, 13¾, 13¾, 14, 14½, 15½)"/[33 (35, 35, 35, 35.5, 37, 39.5)cm] from the beginning, ending after a wrong-side row.

SHAPE RAGLAN

Work fully fashioned raglan decreases (see Notes) every other row 18 (13, 11, 6, 7, 2, 3) times, then every row 10 (20, 26, 36, 38, 48, 50) times—54 (54, 56, 56, 60, 60, 64) stitches remain.

Bind off in pattern.

Front

Work same as the Back until the piece measures approximately 18 (19¼, 20¼, 20¾, 21¼, 22, 23)"/ [45.5 (49, 51.5, 52.5, 54, 56, 58.5)cm] from the beginning, ending after a wrong-side row.

SHAPE NECK

Continue working the fully fashioned raglan decreases same as for the Back, *and at the same time,* bind off the middle 20 (20, 22, 22, 26, 26, 30) stitches.

Continue working the fully fashioned raglan decreases same as for the Back, *and at the same time,* bind off 7 stitches at each neck edge once; bind off 5 stitches at each neck edge once; bind off 3 stitches at each neck edge once; decrease 1 stitch at each neck edge every row twice.

Sleeves *(Make 2)*

With the larger needles, cast on 47 (47, 57, 57, 57, 57, 57) stitches.

Begin the Rib Pattern, and work even until the piece measures approximately 1"/[2.5cm] from the beginning, ending after a wrong-side row.

Work fully fashioned sleeve increases (see Notes) each side every 4 rows 0 (0, 0, 0, 0, 6, 5) times, every 6 rows 0 (0, 0, 0, 6, 14, 15) times, every 8 rows 0 (0, 0, 0, 9, 0, 0) times, every 10 rows 8 (6, 6, 6, 0, 0, 0) times, then every 12 rows 2 (4, 4, 4, 0, 0, 0) times, working new stitches into the Rib Pattern as they accumulate—67 (67, 77, 77, 87, 97, 97) stitches.

Continue even until the piece measures approximately 18 (18½, 18½, 18½, 18½, 18½, 19)"/[45.5 (47, 47, 47, 47, 47, 48.5)cm] from the beginning or to the desired length to the underarm, ending after a wrong-side row.

SHAPE RAGLAN

Work fully fashioned raglan decreases (see Notes) each side every other row 21 (21, 18, 18, 17, 12, 16) times, then every row 4 (4, 12, 12, 18, 28, 24) times—17 stitches remain.

Bind off in pattern.

Finishing

Darn in all remaining yarn tails (page 156).

Block all pieces to the finished measurements (page 156).

Sew 3 of the 4 raglan seams, leaving the back left seam unsewn.

NECKBAND

With the right side facing and smaller needles, pick up and knit 92 (92, 97, 97, 102, 102, 107) stitches around the neck.

Begin with a wrong-side row, and work the Rib Pattern until the neckband measures approximately 1"/[2.5cm].

Bind off *loosely* in pattern.

Sew the last raglan seam, including the side of the neckband.

Sew the side and sleeve seams.

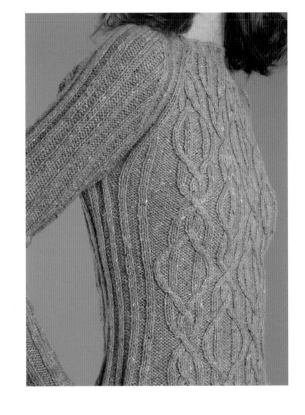

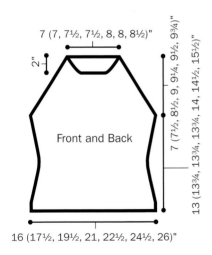

7 (7, 7½, 7½, 8, 8, 8½)"

2"

Front and Back

7 (7½, 8½, 9, 9¼, 9½, 15½)"

13 (13¾, 13¾, 13¾, 14, 14½, 15½)"

16 (17½, 19½, 21, 22½, 24½, 26)"

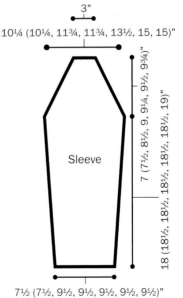

3"

10¼ (10¼, 11¾, 11¾, 13½, 15, 15)"

Sleeve

7 (7½, 8½, 9, 9¼, 9½, 9¾)"

18 (18½, 18½, 18½, 18½, 18½, 19)"

7½ (7½, 9½, 9½, 9½, 9½, 9½)"

CABLE PATTERN

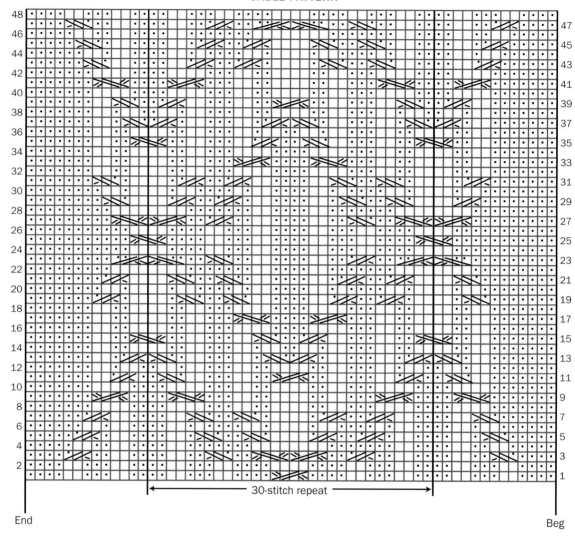

End

Beg

Stitch Key

☐ = K on RS; p on WS

• = P on RS; k on WS

⟋⟋ = Slip next st onto cn and hold in back; k2; p1 from cn

⟍⟍ = Slip 2 sts onto cn and hold in front; p1; k2 from cn

⟋⟋ = Slip 2 sts onto cn and hold in back; k2; k2 from cn

⟍⟍ = Slip 2 sts onto cn and hold in front; k2; k2 from cn

⟋⟋ = Slip 2 sts onto cn and hold in back; k2; p2 from cn

⟍⟍ = Slip 2 sts onto cn and hold in front; p2; k2 from cn

The Weekender

Fully fashioned shaping is essential to this tunic: It's used to create a shapely silhouette, a deep neckline, and perfect-fit sleeve caps.

Skill Level
Intermediate

Sizes
Small (Medium, Large, 1X, 2X, 3X, 4X). Instructions are for the smallest size, with changes for other sizes noted in parentheses as necessary.

Finished Measurements
Bust: 33 (36½, 40, 43, 46, 49, 52½)"/[84 (92.5, 101.5, 109, 117, 124.5, 133.5)cm]
Length: 29 (29½, 29½, 30, 30, 30½, 30½)"/[74 (75, 75, 76, 76, 77.5, 77.5)cm]

Materials
• Lion Brand Yarn's *Superwash Merino Cashmere* (4-medium/worsted weight; 72% superwash merino wool/15% nylon/13% cashmere; each approximately 1.4 oz/[40g] and 87 yds/[80m]): 19 (19, 21, 22, 23, 25, 26) balls of Olive #174 Medium
• Size 8 (5mm) knitting needles or size needed to obtain gauge
• 2 stitch markers
• 2 stitch holders
• Blunt-end yarn needle

Gauge
20 stitches and 28 rows = 4"/[10cm] in the Textured Pattern.
To save time, take time to check gauge.

Stitch Pattern
Textured Pattern (*multiple of 4 + 5 stitches*)
ROW 1 (RS): K1 (selvedge stitch), p3, *k1, p3 ; repeat from the * to the last stitch, k1 (selvedge stitch).
ROW 2: P1 (selvedge stitch), k3, *p1, k3; repeat from the * to the last stitch, p1 (selvedge stitch).
ROW 3: Knit across.
ROW 4: Purl across.
Repeat Rows 1–4 for the pattern.

Fit
Very close-fitting

Figure Flattery

Dozens of vertical lines make this a visually interesting—and figure-flattering—tunic. Add the deep crossover neck, a tiny bit of waist shaping, and a self-belt to accentuate the positive!

Notes

- The instructions include 1 selvedge stitch on each side; these stitches are not included in the finished measurements. For ease in finishing, work the selvedge stitches in stockinette stitch, knitting them on right-side rows and purling them on wrong-side rows.
- For fully fashioned decreases: On right-side rows, k1 (selvedge stitch), work 3 stitches in pattern, ssk, work in pattern to the last 6 stitches, k2tog, work 3 stitches in pattern, k1 (selvedge stitch); on wrong-side rows, p1 (selvedge stitch), work 3 stitches in pattern, p2tog, work in pattern to the last 6 stitches, ssp, work 3 stitches in pattern, p1 (selvedge stitch).
- For fully fashioned increases, work the selvedge stitch, work 4 stitches in pattern, M1-L (page 14), work to the last 5 stitches, M1-R (page 15), work 4 stitches in pattern, work the selvedge stitch; on subsequent rows, work the new stitches into the established Textured Pattern.
- For sweater assembly, refer to the illustration for set-in construction on page 158.

Back

Cast on 85 (93, 101, 109, 117, 125, 133) stitches.

Begin the Textured Pattern, and work even until the piece measures approximately 11¾"/[30cm] from the beginning, ending after a wrong-side row.

DECREASE FOR WAIST

Work fully fashioned decreases (see Notes) each side on the next row, then every 8 rows 3 more times—77 (85, 93, 101, 109, 117, 125) stitches remain.

Continue even until the piece measures approximately 17"/[43cm] from the beginning, ending after a wrong-side row.

INCREASE FOR BUST

Work fully fashioned increases (see Notes) each side on the next row, then every 6 rows 3 more times—85 (93, 101, 109, 117, 125, 133) stitches.

Continue even until the piece measures approximately 20½"/[52cm] from the beginning, ending after a wrong-side row.

SHAPE ARMHOLES

Bind off 4 (4, 8, 8, 8, 12, 12) stitches at the beginning of the next 2 rows. Re-establishing the selvedge stitches at each edge, work fully fashioned decreases

each side every other row 1 (8, 0, 7, 7, 6, 6) times, then every 4 rows 3 (0, 4, 1, 1, 2, 2) times—69 (69, 77, 77, 85, 85, 93) stitches remain.

Continue even until the piece measures 28 (28½, 28½, 29, 29, 29½, 29½)"/[71 (72, 72, 74, 74, 75, 75)cm] from the beginning, ending after a wrong-side row.

SHAPE SHOULDERS

Bind off 4 (4, 5, 5, 6, 6, 7) stitches at the beginning of the next 6 rows, then bind off 5 (5, 6, 6, 7, 7, 8) stitches at the beginning of the next 2 rows—35 stitches remain.

Bind off in pattern.

Front

Work the same as the Back until the piece measures approximately 18½ (19, 19, 19½, 19½, 20, 20)"/[47 (48.5, 48.5, 49.5, 49.5, 51, 51)cm] from the beginning, ending after Row 4 of the Textured Pattern.

Place a marker on each side of the middle 13 stitches.

SHAPE NECK

Work to 1 stitch before the first marker, slip the next stitch on the left-hand needle to the right-hand needle, remove the first marker, slip the same stitch from the right-hand needle back to the left-hand needle, replace the marker, k2tog, work in the established pattern to the next marker; join a second ball of yarn and using the cable cast-on, cast 13 stitches onto the left-hand needle; starting with k1, p3, work Row 1 of the Textured Pattern across the first 12 of these newly cast-on stitches, ssk, place a marker, work in pattern to the end of the row—48 (52, 56, 60, 64, 68, 72) stitches each side.

Working both sides at once with separate balls of yarn, work even at the neck edge for 13 rows *and at the same time,* when the piece measures the same as the Back to underarms, shape armholes same as for Back.

NEXT (NECK-SHAPING) ROW (RS): Work to 1 stitch before the first marker, slip the next stitch on the left-hand needle to the right-hand needle, remove marker, slip the same stitch from the right-hand needle back to the left-hand needle, replace the marker, k2tog, work 12

stitches in pattern; with the second ball of yarn, work 12 stitches in pattern, slip the next stitch on the left-hand needle to the right-hand needle, remove marker, slip the same stitch from the right-hand needle back to the left-hand needle, ssk, replace the marker, work to the end of the row.

Continue shaping the armholes and repeat the last 14 neck-shaping rows twice more—37 (37, 41, 41, 45, 45, 49) stitches remain each side.

Work both sides even until the piece measures approximately 26 (26½, 26½, 27, 27, 27½, 27½)"/ [66 (67.5, 67.5, 68.5, 68.5, 70, 70)cm] from the beginning, ending after a wrong-side row.

NEXT ROW (RS): Work to the marker, then slip the next 13 stitches onto a holder; with the second ball of yarn, work 13 stitches and place them on a holder, remove the marker, work to the end of the row—24 (24, 28, 28, 32, 32, 36) stitches remain each side.

Work 1 row even.

Bind off 3 stitches at each neck edge once; bind off 2 stitches at each neck edge once; then decrease 1 stitch each neck edge every row twice—17 (17, 21, 21, 25, 25, 29) stitches remain each side.

Continue even until the piece measures the same as the Back to shoulders.

SHAPE SHOULDERS
Work same as for the Back.

Sleeves (Make 2)
Cast on 65 (65, 69, 69, 69, 69, 69) stitches.

Work 2 rows of the Textured Pattern.

Work fully fashioned decreases (see Notes) each side on the next row and then every 6 rows 7 more times—49 (49, 53, 53, 53, 53, 53) stitches remain.

Work fully fashioned increases (see Notes) each side on the next row, and then every 4 rows 0 (0, 0, 0, 0, 0, 7) times, every 6 rows 0 (0, 0, 0, 0, 7, 8) times, every 8 rows 0 (0, 0, 0, 9, 4, 0) times, every 10 rows 7 (7, 7, 7, 0, 0, 0) times—65 (65, 69, 69, 73, 77, 85) stitches.

Continue even until the piece measures approximately 18½"/[47cm] from the beginning or the desired sleeve length, ending after a wrong-side row.

SHAPE CAP

Bind off 4 (4, 8, 8, 8, 12, 12) stitches at the beginning of the next 2 rows.

Work fully fashioned decreases (see Notes) each side every other row 14 (12, 8, 7, 11, 5, 13) times, then every 4 rows 0 (2, 4, 5, 3, 7, 3) times—29 stitches remain.

Work 0 (0, 0, 1, 1, 1, 1) row even.

Bind off 3 stitches at the beginning of the next 4 rows—17 stitches remain.

Bind off in pattern.

Finishing

Darn in all remaining yarn tails (page 156).

Block all pieces to the finished measurements (page 156).

Sew the shoulder seams.

NECKBAND

Transfer the 26 front neck stitches from the holders to a knitting needle. With the right side facing and beginning at the right neck edge, work 13 stitches in pattern, pick up and knit 59 stitches around the neckline, work 13 stitches in pattern.

Continue in the established Textured Pattern until the neckband measures approximately 1$\frac{1}{2}$"/[4cm].

Bind off in pattern.

With the right edge under the left edge for a crossover V-neck, whipstitch the 13 cast-on stitches at the bottom of the neck opening to the wrong side of the Front.

Set in the sleeves.

Sew the sleeve seams.

Leaving the lower 6"/[15cm] open for side slits, sew the side seams.

BELT *(OPTIONAL)*

Cast on 11 stitches. Work even in the Textured Pattern (omitting the selvage stitches) until the piece measures approximately 44"/[112cm], ending after Row 2 of the pattern.

Bind off in the pattern.

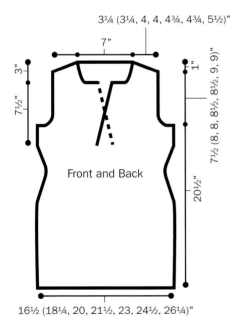

3$\frac{1}{4}$ (3$\frac{1}{4}$, 4, 4, 4$\frac{3}{4}$, 4$\frac{3}{4}$, 5$\frac{1}{2}$)"

7"

3"

7$\frac{1}{2}$"

1"

7$\frac{1}{2}$ (8, 8, 8$\frac{1}{2}$, 8$\frac{1}{2}$, 9, 9)"

Front and Back

20$\frac{1}{2}$"

16$\frac{1}{2}$ (18$\frac{1}{4}$, 20, 21$\frac{1}{2}$, 23, 24$\frac{1}{2}$, 26$\frac{1}{4}$)"

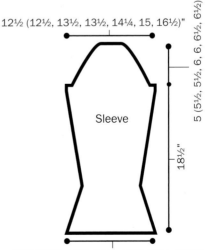

12$\frac{1}{2}$ (12$\frac{1}{2}$, 13$\frac{1}{2}$, 13$\frac{1}{2}$, 14$\frac{1}{4}$, 15, 16$\frac{1}{2}$)"

5 (5$\frac{1}{2}$, 5$\frac{1}{2}$, 6, 6, 6$\frac{1}{2}$, 6$\frac{1}{2}$)"

Sleeve

18$\frac{1}{2}$"

12$\frac{1}{2}$ (12$\frac{1}{2}$, 13$\frac{1}{2}$, 13$\frac{1}{2}$, 13$\frac{1}{2}$, 13$\frac{1}{2}$, 13$\frac{1}{2}$)"

Candace's Shell

This summertime top is, literally, a breeze to make! Its neck and armhole treatments are incorporated into the knitting of the pieces. And all those vertical lines will make anyone look taller and thinner!

Skill Level
Intermediate

Sizes
Small (Medium, Large, 1X, 2X, 3X, 4X). Instructions are for the smallest size, with changes for other sizes noted in parentheses as necessary.

Finished Measurements
Bust: 31 (34, 37, 39, 42, 45, 47)"/[79 (86, 94, 99, 106.5, 114, 119.5)cm]
Length: 23 (23½, 23½, 24, 24, 24½, 24½)"/58.5 (59.5, 59.5, 61, 61, 62, 62)cm]

Materials
- Muench Yarns/Lana Grossa's *Linea Pura Taglia* (6-super bulky weight; 100% mako cotton; each approximately 1¾ oz/[50g] and 99 yds/[90m]): 6 (7, 8, 8, 9, 9, 10) balls of Violet #5  Super Bulky
- Size 13 (9mm) knitting needles or size needed to obtain gauge
- 3 stitch markers
- Blunt-end yarn needle

Gauge
12 stitches and 20 rows = 4"/[10cm] in the Fisherman's Rib.
To save time, take time to check gauge.

Stitch Pattern
Fisherman Rib (*multiple of 2 + 1 stitches*)
ROW 1 (WS): Knit across.
ROW 2: P1, *k1 *in the row below* (page 151), p1; repeat from the * across.
Repeat Rows 1 and 2 for the pattern.

Notes
- For a perfect close fit, this sweater is designed with negative ease. The ribbed pattern will allow the fabric to stretch to fit the body, so knit the size you would normally knit for yourself.
- The instructions include 1 selvedge stitch on each side; these stitches are not included in the finished measurements.

Fit
Very close-fitting

Figure Flattery

This body-conscious design flatters most everyone: its incorporated V-neck and all those vertical ribs seem to elongate the figure. You'll appear taller—and slimmer.

Back

Cast on 49 (53, 57, 61, 65, 69, 73) stitches.

Begin the Fisherman's Rib, and work even until the piece measures approximately 15½"/[39.5cm] from the beginning, ending after a right-side row.

SHAPE ARMHOLES

Bind off 2 (4, 4, 6, 6, 6, 8) stitches at the beginning of the next 2 rows—45 (45, 49, 49, 53, 57, 57) stitches remain.

NEXT ROW (WS): K5, p1, knit to the last 6 stitches, p1, k5.

NEXT ROW: [P1, k1 *in the row below*] twice, p1, sssk, work in pattern to the last 8 stitches, k3tog, [p1, k1 *in the row below*] twice, p1—41 (41, 45, 45, 49, 53, 53) stitches remain.

NEXT ROW: Knit across.

NEXT ROW: P1, *k1 *in the row below,* p1; repeat from the * across.

Repeat the last 4 rows 2 (2, 2, 2, 2, 3, 3) more times—33 (33, 37, 37, 41, 41, 41) stitches remain.

Continue even until the piece measures approximately 20 (20½, 20½, 21, 21, 21½, 21½)"/[51 (52, 52, 53.5, 53.5, 54.5, 54.5)cm] from the beginning, ending after a right-side row.

SHAPE NECK

ROW 1 (WS): K11 (11, 13, 13, 15, 15, 15), p1, k4, k1f&b (page 15), k4, p1, k11 (11, 13, 13, 15, 15, 15)—34 (34, 38, 38, 42, 42, 42) stitches.

ROW 2 (RS): Work 9 (9, 11, 11, 13, 13, 13) stitches in pattern, k3tog, place a marker, [p1, k1 *in the row below*] twice, p1; join a second ball of yarn and [p1, k1 *in the row below*] twice, p1, place a marker, sssk, work in pattern to the end of the row—15 (15, 17, 17, 19, 19, 19) stitches remain each side.

ROW 3: Work even.

ROW 4 (DECREASE ROW): Work in pattern to 3 stitches before the first marker, k3tog, slip the marker, [p1, k1 *in the row below*] twice, p1; for the second side of the neck, with the other ball of yarn, [p1, k1 *in the row below*] twice, p1, slip the marker, sssk, work in pattern to the end of the row—13 (13, 15, 15, 17, 17, 17) stitches remain each side.

Repeat the Decrease Row every other row 3 more times—7 (7, 9, 9, 11, 11, 11) stitches remain each side.

Continue even until the piece measures approximately 22 (22½, 22½, 23, 23, 23½, 23½)"/[56 (57, 57, 58.5, 58.5, 59.5, 59.5)cm] from the beginning, ending after a wrong-side row.

SHAPE SHOULDERS

Bind off 2 (2, 3, 3, 4, 4, 4) stitches at the beginning of the next 4 rows, then bind off 3 stitches at the beginning of the next 2 rows.

Front

Work same as the Back until the piece measures approximately 15½ (16, 16, 16½, 16½, 17, 17)"/[39.5 (40.5, 40.5, 42, 42, 43, 43)cm] from the beginning, ending after a right-side row. Place a marker on the middle stitch.

Continuing the armhole shaping same as for the Back, repeat the Decrease Row every 8 rows 3 more times—7 (7, 9, 9, 11, 11, 11) stitches remain each side.

Continue even until the piece measures approximately 22 (22½, 22½, 23, 23, 23½, 23½)"/[56 (57, 57, 58.5, 58.5, 59.5, 59.5)cm] from the beginning, ending after a wrong-side row.

SHAPE SHOULDERS
Work same as for the Back.

Finishing

Darn in all remaining yarn tails (page 156).

Block both pieces to the finished measurements (page 156).

Sew the shoulder seams.

Sew the side seams.

SHAPE NECK

ROW 1 (WS): Continuing the armhole shaping same as for the Back, work to 5 stitches before the marked center stitch, p1, k4, k1f&b, k4, p1, knit across to the end of the row.

ROW 2 (RS): Continuing the armhole shaping same as for the Back, work in pattern to 8 stitches before the center, k3tog, place a marker, [p1, k1 *in the row below*] twice, p1; join a second ball of yarn and [p1, k1 *in the row below*] twice, p1, place a marker, sssk, work in pattern to the end of the row.

ROWS 3–9: Working both sides at once with separate balls of yarn, continue the armhole shaping same as for the Back, and work 7 rows even at the neck edges.

ROW 10 (DECREASE ROW): Continuing the armhole shaping same as for the Back, work in pattern to 3 stitches before the first marker, k3tog, slip the marker, [p1, k1 *in the row below*] twice, p1; for the second side of the neck, with the other ball of yarn, [p1, k1 *in the row below*] twice, p1, slip the marker, sssk, work in pattern to the end of the row.

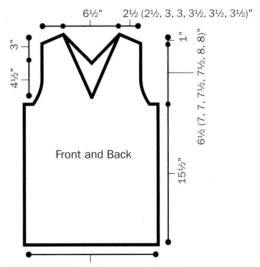

6½"   2½ (2½, 3, 3, 3½, 3½, 3½)"

3"

4½"

1"

6½ (7, 7, 7½, 7½, 8, 8)"

Front and Back

15½"

15½ (17, 18½, 19½, 21, 22½, 23½)"

Winter White

This design uses fully fashioned cabled decreases along the raglan seams. This detail helps draw the eye up to the wearer's face while the cable elongates the torso to create an especially face-flattering sweater.

Skill Level
Intermediate

Sizes
Small (Medium, Large, 1X, 2X, 3X, 4X). Instructions are for the smallest size, with changes for other sizes noted in parentheses as necessary.

Finished Measurements
Bust: 34 (38, 42, 46, 50, 54, 58)"/[86 (96.5, 106.5, 117, 127, 137, 147.5)cm]
Length: 22¼ (22¾, 22¾, 23¼, 23¼, 23¾, 23¾)"/56.5 (58, 58, 59, 59, 60.5, 60.5)cm]

Materials
• Cascade Yarns' *Eco Cloud* (5-bulky weight; 70% undyed merino wool/30% undyed baby alpaca; each approximately 3½ oz/[100g] and 164 yds/ [150m]): 7 (8, 8, 9, 9, 10, 10) hanks of Creme #1801  Bulky
• Size 10 (6mm) knitting needles or size needed to obtain gauge
• Size 10 (6mm) 16"/[40cm] circular needle
• Size 8 (5mm) 16"/[40cm] circular needle
• 2 cable needles
• 2 stitch holders
• 4 stitch markers
• Blunt-end yarn needle

Gauge
16 stitches and 24 rows = 4"/[10cm] in reverse stockinette stitch with the larger needles.
The 22-stitch Cable Panel = 3"/[7.5cm] with the larger needles.
To save time, take time to check gauge.

Stitch Patterns
Rib Pattern (*multiple of 4 stitches*)
ROW 1 (RS): *P1, k2, p1; repeat from the * across.
ROW 2: *K1, p2, k1; repeat from the * across.
Repeat Rows 1 and 2 for the pattern.

Fit
Very close-fitting

Figure Flattery

Bold central cable panels make this sweater especially flattering. Their vertical lines, along with the dimensional decreases at the raglan seams, point directly to the face (and away from anything that might be less than perfect below)!

Reverse Stockinette Stitch (*any number of stitches*)

ROW 1 (RS): Purl across.

ROW 2: Knit across.

Repeat Rows 1 and 2 for pattern.

Cable Panel (*over 22 stitches*)

See the chart.

Notes

- The instructions include 1 selvedge stitch on each side; these stitches are not included in the finished measurements.
- For fully fashioned waist decreases: On right-side rows, p2, p2tog, work in pattern to the last 4 stitches, ssp, p2; on wrong-side rows, k2, ssk, work in pattern to the last 4 stitches, k2tog, k2.
- For raglan pattern: On right-side rows, p2, slip 2 onto a cn and hold in back, k1, k2 from the cn; work in pattern to the last 5 stitches; slip 1 onto a cn and hold in front, k2, k1 from the cn, p2; on wrong-side rows, k2, p3, work in pattern to the last 5 sts; p3, k2.
- For fully fashioned raglan decreases: On right-side rows, do the cable twists while decreasing as follows: p2, slip 2 onto a cn and hold in back, k1, k1 from the cn, ssk to combine the second stitch from the cn with the first stitch on the left-hand needle; work in pattern to the last 6 stitches; slip 1 onto cn #1 and hold in back, slip 1 onto cn #2 and hold in front, k2tog to combine the next stitch on the left-hand needle with the stitch on cn #1, k1, k1 from cn #2, p2; on wrong-side rows, k2, p2, p2tog; work in pattern to the last 6 stitches, ssp, p2, k2.
- For fully fashioned increases, work 4 stitches in pattern, M1 purlwise (page 15), work to the last 4 stitches, M1 purlwise, work 4 stitches in pattern.
- For sweater assembly, refer to the illustration for raglan construction on page 158.

Back

With the larger needles, cast on 78 (86, 94, 102, 110, 118, 126) stitches.

Working Row 1 for each pattern, work the Rib Pattern across 28 (32, 36, 40, 44, 48, 52) stitches, work the Cable Panel across the middle 22 stitches, work the Rib Pattern to the end of the row.

Work even in the established patterns until the piece measures approximately 1½"/[4cm] from the beginning, ending after a wrong-side row, and on the last row, use the M1 technique to increase 1 stitch at the

beginning and the end of the row—80 (88, 96, 104, 112, 120, 128) stitches.

Begin working reverse stockinette stitch on each side of the Cable Panel, and work even until the piece measures approximately 2"/[5cm] from the beginning, ending after a wrong-side row.

DECREASE FOR WAIST

Work fully fashioned decreases (see Notes) each side on the next row and then every 8 rows 3 more times— 72 (80, 88, 96, 104, 112, 120) stitches remain.

Continue even until the piece measures approximately 8"/[20.5cm] from the beginning, ending after a wrong-side row.

INCREASE FOR BUST

Work fully fashioned increases (see Notes) each side on the next row and then every 6 rows 3 more times—80 (88, 96, 104, 112, 120, 128) stitches.

Continue even until the piece measures approximately 12½ (12¾, 12¾, 13, 13, 13¼, 13¼)"/[32 (32.5,

32.5, 33, 33, 33.5, 33.5)cm] from the beginning, ending after a wrong-side row.

SHAPE RAGLAN

Bind off 4 (4, 5, 5, 6, 6, 7) stitches at the beginning of the next 2 rows, then begin the raglan pattern (see Notes) *and at the same time* work fully fashioned raglan decreases (see Notes) each side every 4 rows 5 (3, 0, 0, 0, 0, 0) times, every other row 14 (19, 25, 26, 23, 23, 20) times, then every row 0 (0, 0, 2, 8, 11, 17) times—34 (36, 36, 38, 38, 40, 40) stitches remain.

Work 0 (1, 1, 0, 0, 0, 0) row even.

Place the stitches on a holder. Make a note of which Cable Panel row you ended with.

Front

Work same as the Back.

Sleeves *(Make 2)*

With the larger needles, cast on 36 (36, 36, 40, 40, 40, 40) stitches.

Begin the Rib Pattern, and work even until the piece measures approximately 1½"/4cm] from the beginning, ending after a wrong-side row, and on the last row, use the M1 technique to increase 1 stitch at the beginning and the end of the row—38 (38, 38, 42, 42, 42, 42) stitches.

Begin working reverse stockinette stitch, and work fully fashioned increases each side every 6 rows 0 (0, 0, 0, 0, 6, 14) times, every 8 rows 0 (0, 0, 0, 10, 6, 0) times, every 10 rows 0 (0, 8, 8, 0, 0, 0) times, every 12 rows 0 (2, 0, 0, 0, 0, 0) times, every 14 rows 0 (4, 0, 0, 0, 0, 0) times, every 18 rows 1 (0, 0, 0, 0, 0, 0) time, then every 20 rows 3 (0, 0, 0, 0, 0, 0) times—46 (50, 54, 58, 62, 66, 70) stitches.

Continue even until the piece measures approximately 16 (16½, 16½, 16½, 16½, 17, 17)"/[40.5 (42, 42, 42, 42, 43, 43)cm] from the beginning or to the desired length to underarm, ending after a right-side row.

SHAPE RAGLAN

Bind off 4 (4, 5, 5, 6, 6, 7) stitches at the beginning of the next 2 rows, then begin the raglan pattern *and at the same time* work fully fashioned raglan decreases each side every other row 0 (1, 3, 5, 7,

10, 12) times, every 4 rows 9 (12, 11, 11, 10, 9, 8) times, then every 6 rows 2 (0, 0, 0, 0, 0, 0) times—16 stitches remain.

Work 0 (1, 1, 0, 0, 1, 1) row even.

Bind off all stitches as they present themselves.

Finishing

Darn in all remaining yarn tails (page 156).

Block all pieces to the finished measurements (page 156).

Sew the 4 raglan seams.

NECKBAND

With right side facing and larger circular needle, beginning at the Cable Panel on the Back, work across the Cable Panel in pattern, p6 (7, 7, 8, 8, 9, 9); pick up and knit 14 (16, 16, 14, 14, 16, 16) stitches across the Left Sleeve; work 34 (36, 36, 38, 38, 40, 40) Front stitches in pattern; pick up and knit 14 (16, 16,

14, 14, 16, 16) stitches across the Right Sleeve, p6 (7, 7, 8, 8, 9, 9) remaining Back stitches—96 (104, 104, 104, 104, 112, 112) stitches.

Place markers on either side of the Cable Panel stitches on the Front and the Back.

NECKBAND PATTERN ROUND: [Work the Cable Panel, p2, *k2, p2; repeat from the * to the next marker] twice.

Repeat the last round until the neckband measures approximately 1"/[2.5cm].

Change to the smaller circular needle.

Continue even for an additional 3½"/[9 cm].

Bind off *loosely* in the pattern.

Sew the side and sleeve seams.

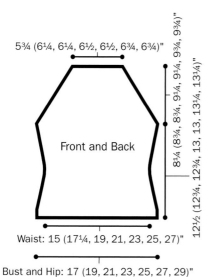

5¾ (6¼, 6¼, 6½, 6½, 6¾, 6¾)"

8¼ (8¾, 8¾, 9¼, 9¼, 9¾, 9¾)"

Front and Back

12½ (12¾, 12¾, 13, 13, 13¼, 13¼)"

Waist: 15 (17¼, 19, 21, 23, 25, 27)"

Bust and Hip: 17 (19, 21, 23, 25, 27, 29)"

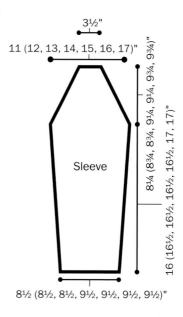

3½"

11 (12, 13, 14, 15, 16, 17)"

8¼ (8¾, 8¾, 9¼, 9¼, 9¾, 9¾)"

Sleeve

16 (16½, 16½, 16½, 16½, 17, 17)"

8½ (8½, 8½, 9½, 9½, 9½, 9½)"

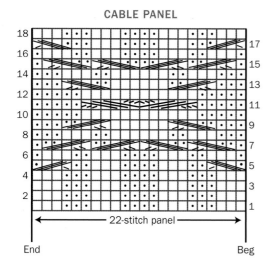

CABLE PANEL

22-stitch panel

End   Beg

Stitch Key

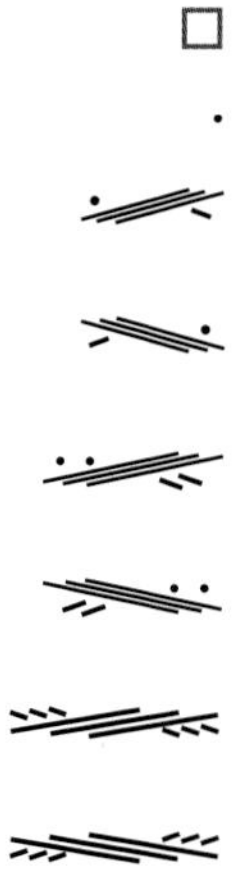

☐ = K on RS; p on WS

• = P on RS; k on WS

⬋ = Slip next stitch onto cn and hold in back; k3; p1 from cn

⬊ = Slip 3 stitches onto cn and hold in front; p1; k3 from cn

⬋ = Slip 2 stitches onto cn and hold in back; k3; p2 from cn

⬊ = Slip 3 stitches onto cn and hold in front; p2; k3 from cn

⬋ = Slip 3 stitches onto cn and hold in back; k3; k3 from cn

⬊ = Slip 3 stitches onto cn and hold in front; k3; k3 from cn

Merino Magic

In this pretty pullover, a line of delicate eyelets frame all the pieces, adding vertical elements which draw the eye upward to flatter nearly every body type.

Skill Level
Intermediate

Sizes
Small (Medium, Large, 1X, 2X, 3X, 4X). Instructions are for the smallest size, with changes for other sizes noted in parentheses as necessary.

Finished Measurements
Bust: 32½ (35, 38, 40½, 44, 47½, 51)"/[82.5 (89, 96.5, 103, 112, 120.5, 129.5)cm]
Length: 22¾ (23, 23¼, 24¼, 24½, 25¼, 25½)"/[58 (58.5, 59, 61.5, 62, 64.5, 65)cm]

Materials
• Trendsetter Yarns' *Merino 8* (4-medium/worsted weight; 100% superwash merino wool; each approximately 1¾ oz/[50g] and 98 yds/[89.5m]): 8 (9, 10, 11, 12, 13, 14) balls of Butter #9940  Medium
• Size 6 (4mm) knitting needles
• Size 8 (5mm) knitting needles or size needed to obtain gauge
• Size 6 (4mm) 16"/[40cm] circular needle
• 4 stitch markers
• Blunt-end yarn needle

Gauge
18 stitches and 24 rows = 4"/[10cm] in stockinette stitch with the larger needles.
To save time, take time to check gauge.

Stitch Patterns
Border Pattern (*multiple of 2 + 1 stitches*)
ROW 1 (RS): Knit across.
ROWS 2–4: As Row 1.
ROW 5: K2, *yarn over, k2tog; repeat from the * to the last stitch, k1.
ROWS 6–10: Purl across.

Special Abbreviation
S2kp2 = Centered double decrease = Slip next 2 stitches at once knitwise, knit the next stitch, pass the 2 slipped stitches over the knit stitch.

Fit
Very close-fitting

Figure Flattery

▲ ▼ ● ▮ ✕

With its slightly shaped silhouette and deliberate designer details, this design can flatter every figure type. Vertical lines begin near the lower edge and continue in the diagonal raglan seams, making the wearer look taller and thinner.

Notes

- The instructions include one selvedge stitch on each side; these stitches are not included in the finished measurements.
- For fully fashioned decreases: On right-side rows, k2, yarn over, s2kp2, knit to the last 5 stitches, s2kp2, yarn over, k2; on wrong-side rows, p3, p2tog, purl to the last 5 stitches, ssp, p3.
- For fully fashioned increases: On right-side rows: k2, yarn over, k2tog, M1-R (page 15), knit to the last 4 stitches, M1-L (page 14), ssk, yarn over, k2.
- For sweater assembly, refer to the illustration for raglan construction on page 158.

Back

With the smaller needles, cast on 67 (73, 79, 85, 91, 97, 105) stitches.

Work the 10-row Border Pattern, and on the last row, use the M1 technique to increase 8 (8, 8, 8, 10, 12, 12) stitches evenly spaced across the row—75 (81, 87, 93, 101, 109, 117) stitches.

SET UP PATTERNS

ROW 1 (EYELET ROW) (RS): Change to the larger needles; k2, yarn over, k2tog, place a marker, knit to the last 4 stitches, place a marker, ssk, yarn over, k2.

ROW 2: Purl across.

Repeat Rows 1 and 2 until the piece measures approximately 3"/[7.5cm] from the beginning, ending after a wrong-side row.

DECREASE FOR WAIST

Continue the eyelets as established, *and at the same time*, work fully fashioned decreases (see Notes) each side on the next row, then every 8 (8, 8, 6, 6, 6, 6) rows twice more—69 (75, 81, 87, 95, 103, 111) stitches remain.

Continue even until the piece measures approximately 7"/[18cm] from the beginning, ending after a wrong-side row.

INCREASE FOR BUST

Work fully fashioned increases (see Notes) each side on the next row, then every 8 (8, 8, 6, 6, 6, 6) rows twice more—75 (81, 87, 93, 101, 109, 117) stitches.

Continue even until the piece measures approximately 14½ (14½, 14½, 15, 15, 15½, 15½)"/[37 (37, 37,

38, 38, 39.5, 39.5)cm] from the beginning, ending after a wrong-side row.

SHAPE RAGLAN AND NECK

Continue in the established pattern and work fully fashioned decreases (see Notes) each side every row 0 (0, 0, 0, 6, 12, 19) times, every other row 6 (11, 17, 20, 18, 16, 13) times, then every 4 rows 6 (4, 1, 0, 0, 0, 0) times, *and at the same time,* when 57 (57, 61, 65, 65, 65, 65) stitches remain, shape the neck as follows: Mark the center 35 (35, 35, 37, 37, 37, 37) stitches. Continuing the fully fashioned decreases, work to the first marker; join a second ball of yarn and bind off to the next marker; work to the end of the row. Working both sides at once with separate balls of yarn, bind off 2 stitches at each neck edge twice.

Continue until all raglan decreases are completed—4 stitches remain on each side.

Work 0 (0, 1, 1, 0, 0, 0) row even.

Bind off the stitches as they present themselves.

Front

Work same as the Back.

Sleeves *(Make 2)*

With the smaller needles, cast on 41 (45, 49, 55, 59, 61, 65) stitches.

Work the 10-row Border Pattern, and on the last row, use the M1 technique to increase 6 (6, 6, 6, 6, 8, 8) stitches evenly spaced across the row—47 (51, 55, 61, 65, 69, 73) stitches.

SET UP PATTERNS

ROW 1 (RS): Change to the larger needles; k2, yarn over, k2tog, place a marker, knit to the last 4 stitches, place a marker, ssk, yarn over, k2.

ROW 2: Purl across.

Repeat Rows 1 and 2 until the piece measures approximately 9"/[23cm] from the beginning, ending after a wrong-side row.

SHAPE RAGLAN

Continue in pattern and work fully fashioned decreases (see Notes) each side every row 0 (0, 0, 0, 0, 2, 5) times, every other row 8 (11, 15, 18, 21, 21, 20) times, then every 4 rows 5 (4, 2, 1, 0, 0, 0) times—21 (21, 21, 23, 23, 23, 23) stitches remain.

Bind off purlwise.

Finishing

Darn in all remaining yarn tails (page 156).

Block all pieces to the finished measurements (page 156).

Sew the 4 raglan seams.

NECKBAND

With the right side facing and the circular needle, beginning at Back left raglan, pick up and knit 133 (133, 133, 145, 145, 145, 145) stitches. Place a marker for the beginning of the round and join.

ROUNDS 1, 3, AND 5: Purl around.

ROUND 2: Knit around.

ROUND 4: *K2tog, yarn over; repeat from the * around.

ROUND 6: Knit, and use k2tog to decrease 20 (20, 20, 22, 22, 22, 22) stitches evenly around—113 (113, 113, 123, 123, 123, 123) stitches remain.

ROUND 7: Purl around.

Bind off knitwise.

Sew the side and sleeve seams.

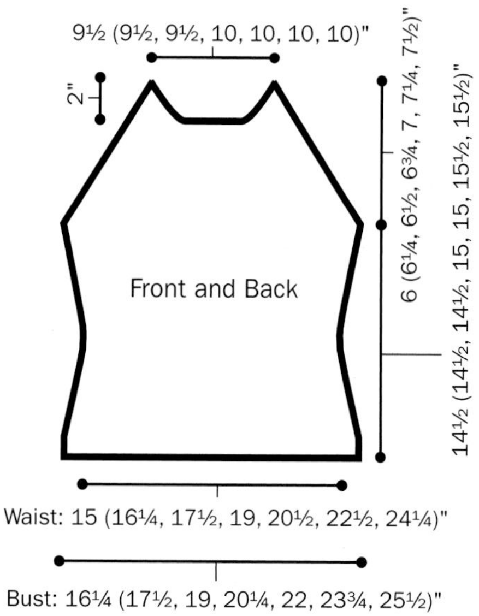

9½ (9½, 9½, 10, 10, 10, 10)"

2"

6 (6¼, 6½, 6¾, 7, 7¼, 7½)"

14½ (14½, 14½, 15, 15, 15½, 15½)"

Front and Back

Waist: 15 (16¼, 17½, 19, 20½, 22½, 24¼)"

Bust: 16¼ (17½, 19, 20¼, 22, 23¾, 25½)"

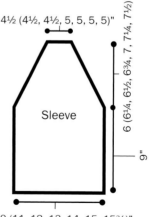

4½ (4½, 4½, 5, 5, 5, 5)"

6 (6¼, 6½, 6¾, 7, 7¼, 7½)"

9"

Sleeve

10 (11, 12, 13, 14, 15, 15¾)"

Marilyn's Crossover Top

Do you think long-sleeved pullovers can't be sexy? Well, think again. Here, intricate cable patterns and fully fashioned decreases are used to create a beautiful, graceful neckline. If you keep their attention near the top of a sweater, no one will notice what you are trying to camouflage below!

Skill Level
Experienced

Sizes
Small (Medium, Large/1X, 2X, 3X/4X). Instructions are for the smallest size, with changes for other sizes noted in parentheses as necessary.

Finished Measurements
Bust: 34 (40, 45, 51, 56½)"/[86 (101.5, 114, 129.5, 143.5)cm]
Length: 22 (22½, 23, 23½, 23½)"/[56 (57, 58.5, 59.5, 59.5)cm]

Materials
• Classic Elite's *Princess* (3-light/DK weight; 40% merino/28% viscose/ 10% cashmere/7% angora/15% nylon; each approximately 1¾ oz/[50g] and 150 yds/[137m]): 9 (10, 11, 12, 13) balls of Pretty Peony #3422 (**3**) Light
• Size 5 (3.75mm) knitting needles
• Size 6 (4mm) knitting needles or size needed to obtain gauge
• Cable needle
• 2 stitch markers
• Blunt-end yarn needle

Gauge
20 stitches and 30 rows = 4"/[10cm] in the Textured Pattern with the larger needles.
The 20-stitch Cable Panel = 2½"/[6.5cm] wide with the larger needles.
To save time, take time to check gauge.

Stitch Patterns
Cabled Rib Pattern (*multiple of 7 + 1 stitches*)
See chart.

Textured Pattern (*multiple of 2 stitches*)
ROW 1 (RS): *P1, k1; repeat from the * across.
ROW 2: Knit across.
Repeat Rows 1 and 2 for the pattern.

Fit
Close-fitting

Figure Flattery

This sweater is a miracle worker: Vertical honeycomb cabled ribs lead up to a flattering empire waist and a face-framing cross-over neckline. Whether you are petite, top-heavy, bottom-heavy, or straight up and down, this dramatic combo is a win-win!

Cable Panels A and B (*over 20 stitches*)
See charts.

Notes

- For fully fashioned increases: work 8 stitches in the Cabled Rib Pattern, M1-R (page 15), work in pattern to the last 8 stitches, M1-L (page 14), work 8 stitches in the Cabled Rib Pattern. On the next row, incorporate new stitches into the pattern as established.
- For fully fashioned decreases: On right-side rows, p1, p2tog, work in pattern to the last 3 stitches, ssp, p1; on wrong-side rows, k1, ssk, work in pattern to the last 3 stitches, k2tog, k1.
- For sweater assembly, refer to the illustration for set-in construction on page 158.

Back

With the smaller needles, cast on 85 (99, 113, 127, 141) stitches.

Begin the Cabled Rib Pattern, and work even until the piece measures approximately 10 (10, 10, 9½, 9½)"/[25.5 (25.5, 25.5, 24, 24)cm] from the beginning, ending after a wrong-side row.

Change to the larger needles, and begin the Textured Pattern.

Continue even in the pattern until the piece measures approximately 13½"/34.5cm] from the beginning, ending after a wrong-side row.

SHAPE ARMHOLES

Bind off 6 (8, 10, 10, 12) stitches at the beginning of the next 2 rows; bind off 2 (3, 4, 6, 8) stitches at the beginning of the next 2 rows; work fully fashioned decreases (see Notes) each side every row 0 (2, 4, 8, 10) times, then every other row 2 (2, 2, 1, 0) times—65 (69, 73, 77, 81) stitches remain.

Continue even until the piece measures approximately 19½ (20, 20½, 21, 21)"/[49.5 (51, 52, 53.5, 53.5)cm] from the beginning, ending after a wrong-side row.

SHAPE NECK

NEXT ROW (RS): Work 6 (8, 10, 12, 14) stitches in pattern; join a second ball of yarn and bind off the middle 53 stitches, work in pattern to the end of the row.

Working both sides at once with separate balls of yarn, decrease 1 stitch at each neck edge once—5 (7, 9, 11, 13) stitches remain each side.

Continue even until the piece measures approximately 21 (21½, 22, 22½, 22½)"/[53.5 (54.5, 56, 57, 57) cm] from the beginning, ending after a wrong-side row.

SHAPE SHOULDERS

Bind off 1 (2, 2, 3, 3) stitches at the beginning of the next 6 rows, then bind off 2 (1, 3, 2, 4) stitch at the beginning of the next 2 rows.

Front

Work same as the Back until the piece measures approximately 10 (10, 10, 9½, 9½)"/[25.5 (25.5, 25.5, 24, 24)cm] from the beginning, ending after Row 4 of the Cabled Rib Pattern.

DIVIDE FOR CROSSOVER NECK

NEXT ROW (RS): Change to the larger needles; working Row 1 of each pattern, work the Textured Pattern across 43 (50, 57, 64, 71) stitches, work Cable Panel A across 20 stitches; join a second ball of yarn and use the cable cast-on technique (page 149) to cast on 41 stitches, work Cable Panel B across the first

20 stitches just cast on, then work the Textured Pattern across 43 (50, 57, 64, 71) stitches—63 (70, 77, 84, 91) stitches each side.

Working both sides at once with separate balls of yarn, work 1 row even in the established patterns and place markers to set off the first and last 44 (51, 58, 65, 72) stitches (the markers will be 1 stitch into each Cable Panel).

DECREASE ROW (RS): Work in pattern to 2 stitches before the first marker, ssp, continue in pattern across this side; for second side, work in pattern to the next marker, p2tog, work in pattern to the end of the row.

Continue the established patterns, and repeat the Decrease Row every other row 14 (12, 10, 7, 7) times, then every 4 rows 13 (15, 17, 20, 20) times, *and at the same time,* when piece measures the same as Back to armholes, shape the armholes same as the Back—25 (27, 29, 31, 33) stitches remain each side.

Continue even until the piece measures the same as the Back to shoulders.

SHAPE SHOULDERS

Work same as for the Back—20 stitches remain each side.

Sew the shoulder seams.

Continue even on the remaining 20 stitches each side until the neckbands, *when slightly stretched,* meet at the center back of the neck.

Bind off.

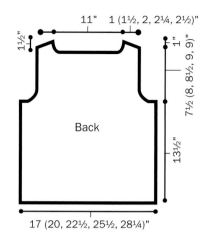

Sleeves (Make 2)

With the smaller needles, cast on 50 stitches.

Begin the Cabled Rib Pattern, and work even until the piece measures approximately 2"/[5cm] from the beginning, ending after Row 4 of the pattern.

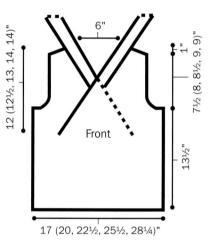

SET UP PATTERNS

NEXT ROW (RS): Change to the larger needles; continue the Cable Rib Pattern across 8 stitches, place a marker, work the Textured Pattern across 34 stitches, place a marker, continue the Cabled Rib Pattern across 8 stitches.

Work fully fashioned increases (see Notes) each side every 6 rows 0 (0, 0, 0, 20) times, every 8 rows 0 (0, 0, 15, 0) times, every 10 rows 0 (0, 6, 0, 0) times, every 12 rows 0 (1, 5, 0, 0) times, every 18 rows 0 (6, 0, 0, 0) times, then every 24 rows 5 (0, 0, 0, 0) times, working new stitches into the Textured Pattern as they accumulate—60 (64, 72, 80, 90) stitches.

Continue even until the piece measures approximately 18½"/[47cm] from the beginning, ending after a wrong-side row.

SHAPE CAP

Bind off 6 (8, 10, 10, 12) stitches at the beginning of the next 2 rows; continuing in the Textured Pattern only, work 1 row even, then work fully

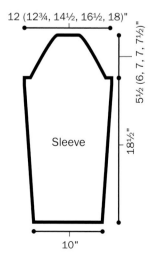

fashioned decreases (see Notes) each side every 4 rows 6 (8, 10, 6, 4) times, then every other row 5 (3, 3, 11, 16) times—26 stitches remain.

Work 0 (0, 0, 0, 1) row even.

Bind off 3 stitches at the beginning of the next 4 rows—14 stitches remain.

Bind off.

CABLED RIB PATTERN

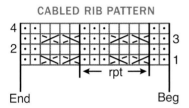

Finishing

Darn in all remaining yarn tails (page 156).

Block all pieces to the finished measurements (page 156).

Sew the sides of neckbands to the back neckline.

Sew the bound-off edges of neckbands together at the back of the Neck.

Sew the cast-on stitches at the center front to the wrong side of the Front.

Set in the sleeves.

Sew the side and sleeve seams.

CABLE PANEL B

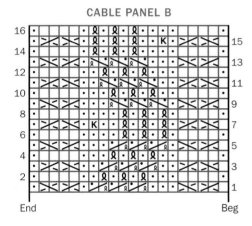

CABLE PANEL A

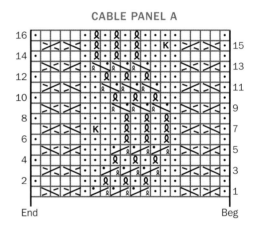

Stitch Key

☐ = K on RS; p on WS

• = P on RS; k on WS

✕ = Right Twist = Slip next st onto cn and hold in back; k1; k1 from cn **OR** k2tog, leaving them on LH needle; insert point of RH needle between these 2 sts and knit the first one again

✕ = Left Twist = Slip next st onto cn and hold in front; k1; k1 from cn **OR** skip first st and knit next st in back loop; then knit the skipped st; slip both sts off LH needle together

= Slip next st onto cn and hold in back; knit next st through back loop; p1 from cn

ℛ = K through back loop on RS; p through back loop on WS

K = Knot = Knit into (front, back, front) of next st, turn; p3, turn; slip 2 sts at once knitwise, k1, p2sso

= Slip next st onto cn and hold in front; p1; k1 from cn through back loop

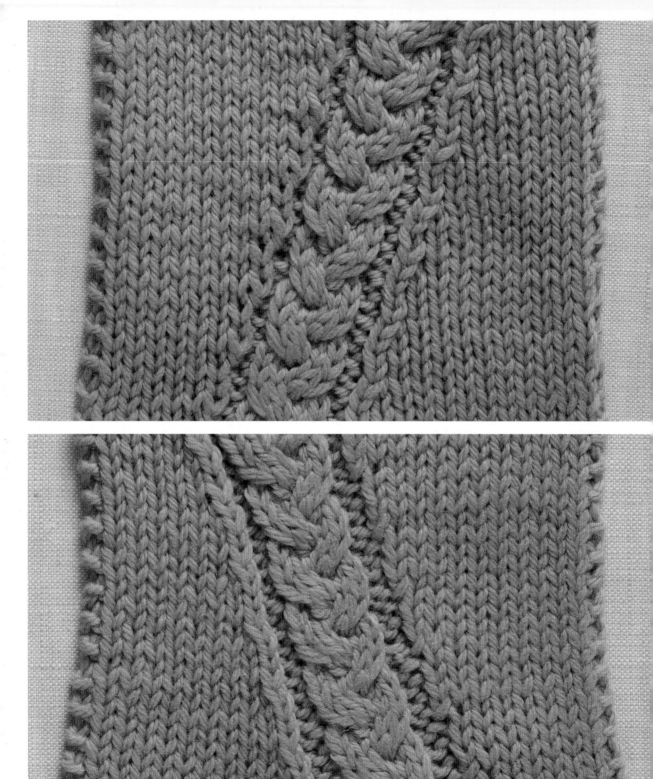

4

Figure
Flatterers

As we've seen, knitters can use fully fashioned shaping to create unique designer elements such as incorporated necklines and armbands into sweaters. Now, let's learn designer tricks using these details to flatter the figure. Regardless of your body type, it is possible to knit to fit and flatter!

Designer Workshop

Knit a Fine Figure

Let's explore ways to flatter every figure type using designer details, from form-fitting bust darts to cleverly positioned vertical elements to strategically placed increases and decreases that create the illusion of shape, even when the sweater silhouette is relatively boxy (read: comfortable)! Refer to the table on page 21 to determine your body type.

▲ The Triangle Body Shape

If you carry most of your weight around your hips and thighs, you'll want to emphasize other areas of your body, especially your face. Here are some designer tips:

Vertical Lift
Use vertical lines to draw the eye up as seen in the illustration below. All that eye movement upward makes the body look taller and slimmer.

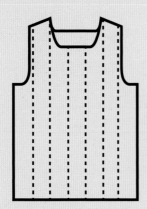

Most Aran-knit sweaters take advantage of the linear arrangement of cable panels in this way. And those two columns of vertical eyelets in Sydney (page 133) have the same figure-flattering effect.

Also, attract attention to a beautifully designed raglan line by incorporating one of the fully fashioned elements explored in Designer Workshop: Enrich Your Knits! (page 58). Notice how the special details in Merino Magic on page 89 flatter so many figure types.

Turn Your Knitting on Its Edge
Everyone knows that horizontal stripes are anything but flattering. Incorporated into a sweater that is knit cuff to cuff, however, they take on a vertical appearance.

Accentuate the Positive
Create attention in areas other than the dreaded hip zone. The Ooh-La-La Skirt (page 45), for example, utilizes flirty flounces at the lower edge to draw the eye to the legs. Better to have folks staring at your sexy gait than at your hips!

As mentioned, raglans are particularly flattering for Triangle-shapes. The diagonal lines point directly to the face and are a wonderful spot to highlight especially decorative fully fashioned decreases, as in Winter White (page 85).

Know All the Angles

To create especially figure-flattering styles, knit strategically placed diagonal lines or sections into your sweaters. They're easy and fun. Here's how:

To create a diagonal going from left to right:
You will be decreasing at the leading edge of the diagonal line or section of stitches and increasing just outside of the trailing edge.

Place a marker one stitch to the left of where you want the leading edge of the diagonal line or section to be, and place another marker immediately to the left of where you want the section to end (the trailing edge).

Then, on right-side rows, work in pattern to 2 stitches before the first marker, work a right-slanting decrease, slip the marker, work to the next marker, slip the marker, work a left-slanting increase, work to the end of the row.

On wrong-side rows, work in pattern to first marker, work a left-slanting increase, slip the marker, work to the next marker, slip the marker, work a right-slanting decrease, work to the end of the row.

The example seen in the swatch above has a right-slanting diagonal braided line six stitches wide with two purl stitches on each side for textural contrast.

To create a diagonal going from right to left:
Place a marker at the spot where you want the trailing edge of the diagonal section and place another marker one stitch to the right of where you want the leading edge to be.

Then, on right-side rows, work in pattern to the first marker, make a right-leaning increase, slip the marker, work to the next marker, slip the marker, work a left-slanting decrease, and work to the end of the row.

On wrong-side rows, work in pattern to 2 stitches before the first marker, work a left-slanting decrease, slip the marker, work to the next marker, slip the marker, work a right-slanting increase, work to the end of the row.

Take a look at the sample swatch above, which has a left-slanting diagonal braided line six stitches wide with two purl stitches on each side for contrast.

Any sort of knit section can be moved this way—from a column of eyelets to ribbing to a solid stockinette panel. Just place stitch markers on either side of the stitches that will be part of the diagonal line and work fully fashioned increases and decreases as described. Choose which directional increase and decrease you'd like to use from those described in the Designer Workshop: Making Simple Stockinette Garments Look Extraordinary (page 24).

Flip Your Triangle Upside Down

Well-placed diagonal lines can minimize the appearance of being bottom heavy.

In the illustration below, the direction of the lines points up and away from the hip area.

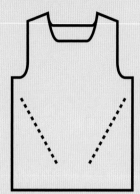

Trompe l'Oeil (page 139) uses this designer trick to flatter the figure. Even though the body of the garment is unshaped, those diagonal lines create the illusion of a tapered silhouette. It's faux-shaping. The diagonals are created by working fully fashioned increases and decreases; for every increase there's a decrease on that same row. When the decrease comes first in the row, the diagonal points toward the right, and when the increase comes first, the diagonal slants to the left.

A series of diagonal lines, with each set pointing up and away from the hips, as seen in the illustration below, is particularly attractive for pear-shaped women.

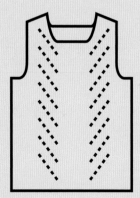

Charlie (page 123) uses these diagonal lines worked in textured stripes. The horizontal effect of the colorwork is broken up by the V at the center of the body.

One common designer trick is to draw attention to the upper area of a garment by using a V-neck. With all the fully fashioned tricks you've learned so far, you can easily place diagonal lines on either side of the neck as seen in the illustration below. It, too, is featured in Trompe l'Oeil (page 139).

Obviously, you'll want to avoid adding any horizontal lines in the lower section of a garment. Contrasting ribbings are definite no-nos. Instead, use a no-edge edge at lower borders. The hemmed detail in Aberdeen (page 49), for example, allows the colorwork pattern to go all the way to the edge and avoids undue attention to the hips. Another idea is to knit a tiny border that rolls to the wrong side. To do: With the public side of the fabric facing, pick up and knit stitches along the lower edge. Then, work a few rows of reverse stockinette, knitting on the wrong side and purling on the right side, before binding off.

Also, avoid sleeves and lower-body edges that end at the widest part of your lower body. If you love a sweater design but need to modify its body or sleeve length, lengthen or shorten the piece before the armhole or sleeve cap shaping begins. Otherwise, you'll interfere with how the sleeves fit into the armholes, causing problems in the finishing. (Not to mention the overall fit!)

Back in the Saddle

Attract attention to the upper third of a sweater by adding saddle shoulders. They act as arrows pointing toward the wearer's face, deflecting emphasis down below.

Puff It Up

Use puffed sleeves to draw the eye up. To knit this type of sleeve cap, work the upper portion of the sleeve cap with few decreases, but be sure to knit to the correct sleeve cap height. Later, when setting in the sleeve, make pinch pleats with the extra fabric at the top or else simply gather it in. Another option is to make rapid decreases across the last few rows before binding off.

▼ The Inverted Triangle Body Shape

If you have broad shoulders or a large bust, use design elements that attract attention to the upper body in a flattering way.

If You've Got It, Flaunt It
Busty women can draw attention to their curves by using fitted bust darts, as seen in Jen (page 127). Just choose your bra cup size and knit the garment to fit.

In Marilyn's Crossover Top (page 93), heavily cabled panels frame the neck opening.

Both designs have high empire waists to emphasize the narrow area just below the bust. Very sexy!

Lighten Up
Deep necklines, such as scoop necks and V-necks, tend to flatter busty women. Opening up the neckline in this way creates the illusion of less weight up top and balances broad shoulders or thick arms. Avoid large lapels. Jacqueline (page 37) has enough of a fold-over lapel to highlight the face without drawing undue attention to the widest part of the body.

Add Some Flare
A-line silhouettes and flared sleeves and cuffs add balance and de-emphasize the upper body. See The Weekender (page 75), for example.

Lengthen the Torso
Women who carry their weight in their upper torso benefit from hemlines that hit lower on the body. Knit your sweaters—and your sleeves—to a longer length. Sweaters tend to be quite flattering if they end at the widest part of the hips, balancing the upper body.

● Round Body Shapes

Women with round body types can use designer tricks to knit flattering sweaters, too.

Paint on a Waist
Use strategically placed increases and decreases to create the illusion of an hourglass figure, as seen here.

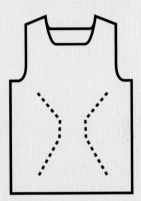

Glamour Girl (page 111) uses this designer trick. Here, subtle waist shaping is accentuated with cables, fooling the eye into seeing much more waist definition.

Emphasize Your Narrowest Spot
Use an empire waistline to draw attention someplace other than your midsection. See Marilyn's Crossover Top (page 93) or Jen (page 127) for examples of this sort of design.

Straight and Narrow
Obviously, round body shapes can benefit from vertical design elements. Cables 'n' Ribs (page 69) uses columns of knit and purl stitches along the sides of the sweater to draw the eye up.

Square It Off
Add square elements, such as square necklines or simple patch pockets to create angular lines.

Diversionary Tactics

Although we tend to idealize the hourglass figure here in the West, folks with round or straight-up-and-down body shapes can get flattering results by attracting attention elsewhere.

Lace ruffles on sleeves, for example, draw the eye to the cuffs and create flattering movement every time the wearer moves. Even a little lace motif near the neck can de-emphasize the waist, bringing attention to the face.

And as we've already seen, an artificially high empire waist highlights the body's narrowest place, deflecting attention from wider areas below, as seen in Marilyn's Crossover Top (page 93) and Jen (page 127).

■ Rectangular Body Shapes

For boyish or athletic figure types, use designer details to flatter.

Go with the Flow
An A-line silhouette creates a feminine look as seen in Angie (page 143). In this design, fully fashioned decreases are neatly incorporated into the lace pattern.

Fake It
Create the illusion of a waist by adding a self-belt, as seen in The Weekender (page 75). Or knit in a faux hourglass motif as described on page 103. The same tricks used to flatter a rounded shape also work here.

The convergence of incorporated neckband and armbands in Candace's Shell (page 81) emphasizes the upper body and creates a beautiful bustline, even if the wearer doesn't have one. (Knit this design for your favorite tween to get lots of brownie points!)

Round It Up
Add a scoop neck to soften the overall look.

⧗ Hourglass Body Shapes

Let's face it: Folks with hourglass figures don't need a lot of help to look good. Following are suggestions to improve on perfection.

Curves Ahead
- Obviously, designs with body-conscious style are ideal. Choose sweaters with waist shaping. Or add a belt to cinch in the waist.

- Use fully fashioned increases and decreases to emphasize the waist as seen in Glamour Girl (page 111).

Keep It Light
Don't overwhelm the delicate hourglass shape by wearing garments that are droopy or bulky.

Special Design Considerations

Plus-Size Body Types

Larger women might have any of the body shapes listed in this book (triangle or inverted triangle, etc.) but on a bigger scale. Their sweaters possess a larger canvas and provide lots of opportunity for designer elements.

- Use diagonal lines created by fully fashioned increases and decreases to paint an abstract geometric pattern as seen here. The pattern guides the eye to the face of the wearer, detracting from any figure flaws below.

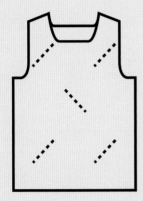

- The angular elements in Angled Ribs (page 117) work the same way. There's lots of eye movement in the design.

- For a plus-size jacket or cardigan, make sure your buttons aren't too small in circumference. Larger ones will balance the overall look.

- Choose garments with design elements that bisect the body, such as Marie (page 107). The lace panels travel from the hips directly toward the V-neck opening, minimizing width.

- The last thing a plus-size frame needs is more girth. For the most flattering results, choose lighter-weight yarns that knit at a smaller gauge. Think about it: Bulky yarns can add an inch or more to the circumference of a sweater!

Petite Body Types

With a more diminutive canvas to paint on, designer elements in petite garments must be diminished in size or else they might be overwhelming to the wearer.

- Pocket widths in Jacqueline (page 37), for example, might be reduced to 17 stitches across instead of 21 stitches.

- Collar sizes, too, should be reduced. In Orvieto (page 65), the jacket will flatter a petite frame better if the collar stops at 4½"/[11.5cm] rather than 5½"/[14cm].

- Of course, many petite figures have short waists, so sweaters must be shorter in length. Take care to remove the extra length below the armhole shaping. Otherwise, the sleeves won't fit into the armholes.

- Add as many vertical elements as possible to elongate the body, from a V-neck to raglan shaping.

Are you tired of knitting sweaters that don't suit your body? Would you like to knit to fit? Use fully fashioned details to create garments that work for you and your body type! The eight projects that follow are designed to fit and flatter many individual shapes. Just look for the style icon to choose the best ones for your figure.

Marie

With its lace panels traveling across the stockinette ground, this design is interesting to look at both coming and going. And, since the Front and Back have different design details toward the top, it's lots of fun to knit.

Skill Level
Intermediate

Sizes
Small (Medium, Large, 1X, 2X, 3X). Instructions are for the smallest size, with changes for other sizes noted in parentheses as necessary.

Finished Measurements
Bust: 35 (39, 43, 47, 51, 55)"/[89 (99, 109, 119.5, 129.5, 139.5)cm]
Length: 23 (23½, 24, 24½, 24½, 25)"/[58.5 (59.5, 61, 62, 62, 63.5)cm]

Materials
• Cascade Yarns' *Sierra* (4-medium/worsted weight; 80% pima cotton/20% wool; each approximately 3½ oz/[100g] and 191 yds/[174.5m]): 6 (7, 8, 9, 10, 11) hanks of Lilac #1215 (4) Medium
• Size 5 (3.75mm) knitting needles
• Size 7 (4.5mm) knitting needles or size needed to obtain gauge
• 4 stitch markers
• 2 stitch holders
• Blunt-end yarn needle

Gauge
18 stitches and 25 rows = 4"/[10cm] in stockinette stitch with the larger needles.
10-stitch Lace Panels = 1¾"/[4.5cm] wide with the larger needles.
To save time, take time to check gauge.

Stitch Patterns
Rib Pattern (*multiple of 2 stitches*)
ROW 1 (RS): *K1, p1; repeat from the * across.
PATTERN ROW: As Row 1.

Stockinette Stitch (*any number of stitches*)
ROW 1 (RS): Knit across.
ROW 2: Purl across.
Repeat Rows 1 and 2 for pattern.

Lace Panel A (*over 10 stitches*)
See chart.

Lace Panel B (*over 10 stitches*)
See chart.

Notes

- For fully fashioned decreases: On right-side rows, k2, ssk, work in pattern to the last 4 stitches, k2tog, k2; on wrong-side rows, p2, p2tog, work in pattern to the last 4 stitches, ssp, p2.
- For fully fashioned increases, k2, M1-R, work in pattern to the last 2 stitches, M1-L, k2.
- For sweater assembly, refer to the illustration for set-in construction on page 158.

Back

With the smaller needles, cast on 84 (94, 102, 110, 120, 128) stitches.

Begin the Rib Pattern, and work even until the piece measures approximately 1½"/[4cm] from the beginning, ending after a wrong-side row.

SET UP PATTERNS AND BEGIN INWARD ANGLES

ROW 1 (RS): Change to larger needles; working Row 1 of each pattern, k5 (5, 5, 5, 5, 6), place a marker, work Lace Panel A across 10 stitches, place a marker, k54 (64, 72, 80, 90, 96), place a marker, work Lace

Panel B across 10 stitches, place a marker, k5 (5, 5, 5, 5, 6).

ROW 2: Work stockinette stitch outside the markers and the Lace Panels between them.

ROW 3 (RS): Knit to the first marker, yarn over, slip the marker, work Lace Panel A, slip the marker, ssk, knit to 2 stitches before the next marker, k2tog, slip the marker, work Lace Panel B, slip the marker, yarn over, knit to the end of the row.

Maintaining the established patterns, repeat Row 3 every 4 rows 19 (14, 10, 6, 1, 0) times, every other row 6 (16, 24, 32, 42, 47) times, then work even in stockinette stitch and the Lace Panels to the end; *at the same time*, when the piece measures approximately 14½"/[37cm] from the beginning, ending after a wrong-side row, shape the armholes as follows:

SHAPE ARMHOLES

Bind off 4 (6, 7, 8, 9, 9) stitches at the beginning of the next 2 rows; bind off 2 (2, 2, 3, 4, 4) stitches at the beginning of the next 2 rows; work fully fashioned decreases (see Notes) each side every row 0 (0, 0, 0, 2, 4) times, then every other row 6 (7, 8, 8, 7, 7) times—60 (64, 68, 72, 76, 80) stitches remain. Continue even in pattern until the piece measures approximately 21 (21½, 22, 22½, 22½, 23)"/[53.5 (54.5, 56, 57, 57, 58.5)cm] from the beginning, ending after a wrong-side row.

SHAPE NECK

K5 (7, 9, 11, 13, 15), join a second ball of yarn and bind off the middle 50 stitches, k5 (7, 9, 11, 13, 15). Work both sides at once with separate balls of yarn until the piece measures approximately 22 (22½, 23, 23½, 23½, 24)"/[56 (57, 58.5, 59.5, 59.5, 61)cm] from the beginning, ending after a wrong-side row.

SHAPE SHOULDERS

Bind off 2 (2, 3, 4, 4, 5) stitches at the beginning of the next 4 rows, then bind off 1 (3, 3, 3, 5, 5) stitches at the beginning of the next 2 rows.

Front

Work same as the Back until the piece measures approximately 17"/[43cm] from the beginning, ending after a wrong-side row. Note: All Inward Angles rows should be complete.

SHAPE NECK

DECREASE ROW (RS): Continuing armhole decreases if necessary, knit to 2 stitches before the first marker, k2tog, slip the marker, work 10 stitches in pattern, k1; join a second ball of yarn and k1, work 10 stitches in pattern, slip the marker, ssk, knit to the end of the row.

Working both sides at once with separate balls of yarn and working 1 stitch at each neck edge in garter stitch, repeat the Decrease Row every other row 8 more times, then every 4 rows 5 times—16 (18, 20, 22, 24, 26) stitches remain each side.

Continue even, if necessary, until the piece measures the same as the Back to shoulders, ending after a wrong-side row.

SHAPE SHOULDERS

Work same as for Back—11 stitches remain each side. Put these stitches onto holders.

Sleeves *(Make 2)*

With the smaller needles, cast on 44 (44, 44, 48, 48, 48) stitches.

Begin the Rib Pattern, and work even until the piece measures approximately 1½"/[4cm] from the beginning, ending after a wrong-side row.

SET UP PATTERNS

NEXT ROW (RS): Change to the larger needles; k17 (17, 17, 19, 19, 19), place a marker, work Row 1 of Lace Panel A over 10 stitches, place a marker, knit to the end of the row.

Working stockinette stitch outside the markers and Lace Panel A between them, work fully fashioned increases (see Notes) each side every 4 rows 0 (0, 0, 0, 0, 4) times, every 6 rows 0 (0, 0, 0, 6, 14) times, every 8 rows 0 (0, 0, 0, 8, 0) times, every 10 rows 0 (0, 10, 10, 0, 0) times, every 12 rows 0 (6, 0, 0, 0, 0) times, every 14 rows 0 (2, 0, 0, 0, 0) times, every 16 rows 4 (0, 0 , 0, 0, 0) times, then every 18 rows 2 (0, 0, 0 , 0, 0) times—56 (60, 64, 68, 76, 84) stitches.

Continue even until the piece measures approximately 18½"/[47cm] from the beginning, ending after a wrong-side row.

SHAPE CAP

Bind off 4 (6, 7, 8, 9, 9) stitches at the beginning of the next 2 rows, then work fully fashioned decreases (see Notes) each side every 4 rows 0 (2, 3, 3, 0, 0) times, every other row 13 (11, 11, 12, 18, 18) times, then every row 0 (0, 0, 0, 0, 4) times—22 stitches remain.

Work 1 (1, 0, 1, 1, 0) row even.

Bind off 2 stitches at the beginning of the next 4 rows—14 stitches remain.

Bind off.

Finishing

Darn in all remaining yarn tails (page 156).

Block all pieces to the finished measurements (page 156).

Sew the shoulder seams.

NECKBANDS

Transfer the 11 Front neck stitches from each side to knitting needles; continue even on each side until the neckbands, *when slightly stretched*, meet at the center back of the neck.

Sew the sides of neckbands to the back neckline.

Sew the bound-off edges of neckbands together at the back of the neck.

Set in the sleeves.

Sew the side and sleeve seams.

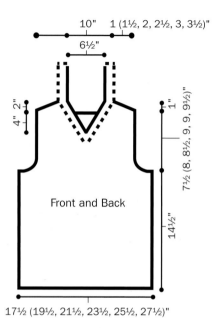

Front and Back

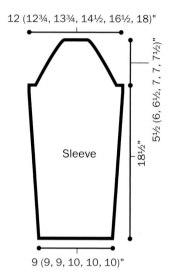

Sleeve

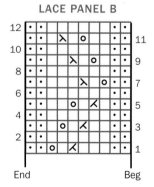

LACE PANEL B

End   Beg

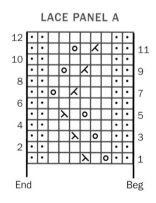

LACE PANEL A

End   Beg

Stitch Key

☐ = K on RS; p on WS

• = P on RS; k on WS

o = Yarn over

⼂ = K2tog

⋋ = Ssk

Glamour Girl

In this clever design, little rope cables create the illusion of an hourglass figure even if you don't have one of your own. Its picot hems are the perfect simple edge treatment, unobtrusive yet refined.

Skill Level
Experienced

Sizes
Small (Medium, Large, 1X, 2X, 3X, 4X). Instructions are for the smallest size, with changes for other sizes noted in parentheses as necessary.

Finished Measurements
Bust: 33 (35, 37, 40, 44, 48, 52)"/[84 (89, 94, 101.5, 112, 122, 132)cm]
Length: 19½ (20½, 20½, 21½, 22, 23, 23)"/[49.5 (52, 52, 54.5, 56, 58.5, 58.5)cm]

Materials
- Westminster Fibers/Nashua Handknits' *Grand Opera* (3-light/DK weight; 86% merino wool/9% viscose/5% metallized [sic] polyester; each approximately 1¾ oz/[50g] and 128 yds/[117m]): 8 (9, 11, 12, 14, 15, 16) balls of Gold #5036 (3) Light
- Size 5 (3.75mm) knitting needles or size needed to obtain gauge
- Size 5 (3.75mm) 16"/[40cm] circular knitting needle
- Size 3 (3.25mm) knitting needles
- Size 3 (3.25mm) 16"/[40cm] circular knitting needle
- Size 3 (3.25mm) 24"/[60cm] circular knitting needle
- Cable needle
- 4 stitch markers
- Blunt-end yarn needle

Gauge
24 stitches and 32 rows = 4"/[10cm] in stockinette stitch with the larger needles.
To save time, take time to check gauge.

Stitch Patterns
Stockinette Stitch (*any number of stitches*)
ROW 1 (RS): Knit across.
ROW 2: Purl across.
Repeat Rows 1 and 2 for the pattern.

Right Cable Panel (*over 10 stitches*)
See chart.

Left Cable Panel (*over 10 stitches*)
See chart.

Fit
Very close-fitting

Figure Flattery

▲ ▽ ● ■ X

Fully fashioned increases and decreases force the little rope cables on the front and back of this sweater in and out to create the illusion of an hourglass waist (whether you've actually got one or not!). And picot-hemmed edges are subtle and refined and do not attract attention where you don't need it.

Notes

- For fully fashioned body decreases: Work to the second marker, slip the marker, k1, ssk, work to 3 stitches before the next marker, k2tog, k1, slip the marker, work to the end of the row.
- For fully fashioned body increases: Work to the second marker, slip the marker, k1, M1-L (page 14), work to 1 stitch before the next marker, M1-R (page 15), k1, slip the marker, work to the end of the row.
- For fully fashioned sleeve increases: K2, M1-R, knit to the last 2 stitches, M1-L, k2.
- For fully fashioned armhole and sleeve cap decreases: On right-side rows, k2, ssk, knit to the last 4 stitches, k2tog, k2; on wrong-side rows, p2, p2tog, purl to the last 4 stitches, ssp, p2.
- For fully fashioned neck decreases: On the right-hand side of the neck, knit to the last 3 stitches before the neck edge, k2tog, k1; on the left-hand side of the neck, k1, ssk, knit to the end of the row.
- For sweater assembly, refer to the illustration for set-in construction on page 158.

Back

With the smaller needles, use the provisional cast-on method (page 151) to cast on 99 (105, 111, 121, 133, 145, 157) stitches.

Begin stockinette stitch, and work even until the piece measures approximately 1"/[2.5cm] from the beginning, ending after a wrong-side row.

TURNING ROW FOR HEM

NEXT ROW (RS): Change to the larger needles; k1, *yarn over, k2tog; repeat from the * across.

NEXT ROW: Continue stockinette stitch until the piece measures approximately 1"/[2.5cm] from the turning row, ending after a wrong-side row.

FOLD UP HEM

Carefully remove the crocheted chain from the provisional cast-on, and transfer the stitches onto the 24" circular needle as they are released from the chain. Fold the hem in half with the knit side on the outside, and hold the circular knitting needle behind the main knitting needle. With both needles in your left hand, k2tog, combining 1 stitch from the main needle and 1 stitch from the circular knitting needle, all the way across the row.

Continue even until the piece measures approximately 1¼"/[3cm] from the turning row, ending after a wrong-side row.

SET UP PATTERNS

ROW 1 (RS): K15 (16, 18, 23, 28, 32, 38), place a marker, k1, p3, [k1, M1 knitwise] twice, p3, place a marker, k51 (55, 57, 57, 59, 63, 63), place a marker, p3, [k1, M1 knitwise] twice, p3, k1, place a marker, knit to the end of the row—103 (109, 115, 125, 137, 149, 161) stitches.

ROW 2: Knit the knit stitches and purl the purl stitches.

ROW 3: Working Row 1 of each Cable Panel, knit to the first marker, slip the marker, k1, work the Right Cable Panel across 10 stitches, slip the marker, knit to the next marker, slip the marker, work the Left Cable Panel across 10 stitches, k1, slip the marker, knit to the end of the row.

ROW 4: Knit the knit stitches and purl the purl stitches.

DECREASE FOR WAIST

Work fully fashioned decreases (see Notes) every other row 0 (2, 4, 4, 8, 8) times, every 4 rows 4 (6, 5, 5, 6, 4, 4) times, then every 6 rows 2 (0, 0, 0, 0, 0, 0) times—91 (93, 97, 107, 117, 125, 137) stitches remain.

Continue even until the piece measures approximately 4¾ (5½, 5½, 6, 6¼, 6½, 6¾)"/[12 (14, 14, 15, 16, 16.5, 17)cm] from the turning row, ending after a wrong-side row.

INCREASE FOR BUST

Work fully fashioned increases (see Notes) every 6 rows 2 (0, 0, 0, 0, 0, 0) times, every 4 rows 4 (6, 5, 5, 6, 4, 4) times, then every other row 0 (2, 4, 4, 4, 8, 8) times—103 (109, 115, 125, 137, 149, 161) stitches.

NEXT ROW (RS): Work to the first marker, slip the marker, k1, p3, [k2tog] twice, work to the third marker, slip the marker, p3, [k2tog] twice, work to the end of the row—99 (105, 111, 121, 133, 145, 157) stitches.

NEXT ROW (WS): Purl across, removing the markers.

Continue even in stockinette stitch until the piece measures approximately 11½ (12, 12, 12½, 13, 13½, 13½)"/[29 (30.5, 30.5, 32, 33, 34.5, 34.5)cm] from the turning row, ending after a wrong-side row.

SHAPE ARMHOLES

Bind off 6 (7, 8, 9, 10, 11, 12) stitches at the beginning of the next 2 rows; bind off 2 (2, 2, 3, 4, 5, 6) stitches at the beginning of the next 2 rows; work fully fashioned armhole decreases (see Notes) every other row 0 (0, 0, 0, 4, 7, 10) times, every 4 rows 3 (2, 2, 4, 2, 1, 0) times, then every 6 rows 0 (1, 1, 0, 0, 0, 0) times—77 (81, 85, 89, 93, 97, 101) stitches remain.

Continue even until the piece measures approximately 18 (19, 19, 20, 20½, 21½, 21½)"/[45.5 (48.5, 48.5, 51, 52, 54.5, 54.5)cm] from the turning row, ending after a wrong-side row.

SHAPE NECK

NEXT ROW (RS): K20 (22, 24, 26, 28, 30, 32), join a second ball of yarn and bind off the middle 37 stitches, knit to the end of the row.

Working both sides at once with separate balls of yarn, work 1 row even.

NEXT ROW: Work fully fashioned neck decreases at each neck edge—19 (21, 23, 25, 27, 29, 31) stitches remain each side.

Work both sides even until the piece measures approximately 18½ (19½, 19½, 20½, 21, 22, 22)"/ [47 (49.5, 49.5, 52, 53.5, 56, 56)cm] from the beginning, ending after a wrong-side row.

SHAPE SHOULDERS

Bind off 5 (5, 6, 6, 7, 7, 8) stitches at the beginning of the next 6 rows, then bind off 4 (6, 5, 7, 6, 8, 7) stitches at the beginning of the next 2 rows.

Front

Work the same as the Back until the piece measures approximately 13 (14, 14, 15, 15½, 16½, 16½)"/ 33 (35.5, 35.5, 38, 39.5, 42, 42)cm] from the turning row, ending after a wrong-side row. Mark the middle 17 stitches.

SHAPE NECK

NEXT ROW (RS): Continue armhole decreases same as the Back, *and at the same time,* work to the marked stitches, join a second ball of yarn and bind off 17 stitches, work to the end of the row.

Working both sides at once with separate balls of yarn, bind off 4 stitches at each neck edge twice; bind off 2 stitches each neck edge once; work a fully fashioned neck decrease at each neck edge once—19 (21, 23, 25, 27, 29, 31) stitches remain each side.

Complete same as the Back.

Sleeves (Make 2)

With the smaller needles, use the provisional cast-on method to cast on 57 (61, 65, 69, 75, 83, 89) stitches.

Begin working stockinette stitch, and work even until the piece measures approximately 1"/[2.5cm] from the beginning, ending after a wrong-side row.

TURNING ROW FOR HEM

NEXT ROW (RS): Change to the larger needles; k1, *yarn over, k2tog; repeat from the * across.

NEXT ROW: Continue stockinette stitch until the piece measures approximately 1"/[2.5cm] from the turning row, ending after a wrong-side row.

FOLD UP HEM

Carefully remove the crocheted chain from the provisional cast-on, and transfer the stitches onto the

SHAPE CAP

Bind off 6 (7, 8, 9, 10, 11, 12) stitches at the beginning of the next 2 rows, then work fully fashioned sleeve cap decreases (see Notes) every 4 rows 4 (5, 6, 6, 5, 3, 0) times, then every other row 7 (7, 5, 7, 10, 15, 21) times—35 stitches remain.

Bind off 3 stitches at the beginning of the next 4 rows—23 stitches remain.

Bind off.

Finishing

Darn in all remaining yarn tails (page 156).

Block all pieces to the finished measurements (page 156).

Sew the shoulder seams.

NECKBAND

With the right side facing, using the larger circular needle and beginning at the left back neck, pick up and knit 140 stitches evenly spaced around the neckline. Place a marker for the beginning of the round and join.

Knit 6 rounds.

NEXT ROUND: *K2tog, yarn over; repeat from the * around.

Change to the smaller circular needle, and knit 7 rounds.

Fold neckband in half to the wrong side and *loosely* sew into place.

Set in the sleeves.

Sew the side and sleeve seams.

16" circular needle as they are released from the chain. Fold the hem in half with the knit side on the outside, and hold the circular knitting needle behind the main knitting needle. With both needles in your left hand, k2tog, combining 1 stitch from the main needle and 1 stitch from the circular knitting needle, all the way across the row.

Continue even until the piece measures approximately 1¼"/[3cm] from the turning row, ending after a wrong-side row.

Work fully fashioned sleeve increases (see Notes) each side every 12 rows 4 (2, 0, 0, 0, 0, 0) times, every 14 rows 2 (4, 0, 0, 0, 0, 2) times, every 16 rows 0 (0, 0, 3, 1, 0, 4) times, every 18 rows 0 (0, 0, 2, 4, 4, 0) times, then every 20 rows 0 (0, 4, 0, 0, 1, 0) times—69 (73, 73, 79, 85, 93, 101) stitches.

Continue even until the piece measures approximately 11½ (12, 12, 12½, 13, 13½, 13½)"/[29 (30.5, 30.5, 32, 33, 34.5, 34.5)cm] from the turning row, ending after a wrong-side row.

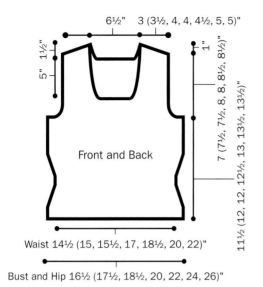

6½" 3 (3½, 4, 4, 4½, 5, 5)"

1½"

5"

1"

7 (7½, 7½, 8, 8, 8½, 8½)"

Front and Back

11½ (12, 12, 12½, 13, 13½, 13½)"

Waist 14½ (15, 15½, 17, 18½, 20, 22)"

Bust and Hip 16½ (17½, 18½, 20, 22, 24, 26)"

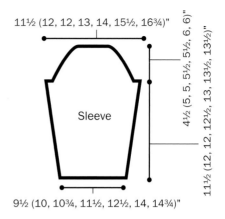

11½ (12, 12, 13, 14, 15½, 16¾)"

4½ (5, 5, 5½, 5½, 6, 6)"

Sleeve

11½ (12, 12, 12½, 13, 13½, 13½)"

9½ (10, 10¾, 11½, 12½, 14, 14¾)"

LEFT CABLE PANEL

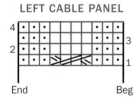

End   Beg

RIGHT CABLE PANEL

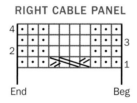

End   Beg

Stitch Key

☐ = K on RS; p on WS

• = P on RS; k on WS

= Slip 2 sts onto cn and hold in back; k2; k2 from cn

= Slip 2 sts onto cn and hold in front; k2; k2 from cn

Angled Ribs

Well-placed increases and decreases create this flattering sweater and make it especially interesting to knit. Use those stitch markers to your advantage, being careful to increase and make yarn overs where specified.

Skill Level
Experienced

Sizes
Small (Medium, Large, 1X, 2X, 3X). Instructions are for the smallest size, with changes for other sizes noted in parentheses as necessary.

Finished Measurements
Bust (*unstretched*): 31½ (35½, 39, 43, 47, 50)"/[80 (90, 99, 109, 119.5, 127)cm]
Length (*at the side seam*): 24 (24, 24½, 24½, 25½, 25½)"/[61 (61, 62, 62, 65, 65)cm]

Materials
- Skacel Collection/Zitron's *Ecco* (3-light DK weight; 100% merino wool; each approximately 1¾ oz/[50g] and 134 yds/[110m]): 13 (14, 15, 16, 17, 18) balls of Terracotta #137  Light
- Size 4 (3.5mm) knitting needles
- Size 5 (3.75mm) knitting needles or size needed to obtain gauge
- 4 stitch markers
- Blunt-end yarn needle

Gauge
34 stitches and 32 rows = 4 /[10cm] in the Rib Pattern, *unstretched*, with the larger needles.
To save time, take time to check gauge.

Stitch Patterns
Rib Pattern (*multiple of 4 + 2 stitches*)
ROW 1 (RS): K2, *p2, k2; repeat from the * across.
ROW 2: P2, *k2, p2; repeat from the * across.
Repeat Rows 1 and 2 for the pattern.

Angled Rib Pattern

ROW 1 (RS): Maintaining the established pattern, work 6 (14, 22, 30, 30, 38) stitches, place a marker, ssp, work to the first center marker, yarn over, slip the marker, work to the second center marker, slip the marker, yarn over, work to the last 8 (16, 24, 32, 32, 40) stitches, p2tog, place a marker, work to the end of the row.

ROW 2: Maintaining the established pattern, work to 1 stitch before the first center marker, p1, slip the marker, work to the second center marker, slip the marker, p1, work to the end of the row.

ROW 3: Maintaining the established pattern, work to the first side marker, slip the marker, k2tog, work to the first center marker, yarn over, slip the marker, work to the second center marker, slip the marker, yarn over, work to 2 stitches before the second side marker, ssk, slip the marker, work to the end of the row.

ROW 4: As Row 2.

ROW 5: As Row 3.

ROW 6: Maintaining the established pattern, work to 1 stitch before the first center marker, k1, slip the marker, work to the second center marker, slip the marker, k1, work to the end of the row.

ROW 7: As Row 1.

ROW 8: As Row 6.

Repeat Rows 1–8 for the pattern.

Notes

- For a close fit, this sweater is designed with negative ease. The ribbed pattern will allow the fabric to stretch to fit the body, so knit the size you would normally knit for yourself.
- The stitch count will remain constant on every row until the armholes, and then it will remain constant until the beginning of the neck shaping.
- For fully fashioned increases: K6, M1-R (page 15), work to the last 6 stitches, M1-L (page 14), k6.
- The smaller needles are used only for the neckband.
- For sweater assembly, refer to the illustration for square indented drop-shoulder construction (page 158).

Back

With the larger needles, cast on 134 (150, 166, 182, 198, 214) stitches.

Work 2 rows of the Rib Pattern, placing a marker on either side of the middle 10 stitches.

Begin Angled Rib Pattern, and work until the piece measures approximately 15½ (15½, 15½, 15½, 16, 16)"/[39.5 (39.5, 39.5, 39.5, 40.5, 40.5)cm] from the beginning, ending after a wrong-side row.

SHAPE ARMHOLES

Continuing the established pattern, bind off 5 (13, 21, 29, 29, 37) stitches at the beginning of the next 2 rows—124 (124, 124, 124, 140, 140) stitches remain.

Working the first and last stitches in stockinette stitch, continue even in the Angled Rib Pattern until the piece measures approximately 17 (17, 17½, 17½, 17½, 17½)"/[43 (43, 44.5, 44.5, 44.5, 44.5)cm] from the beginning, ending after a wrong-side row. Move the center markers to either side of the middle 12 stitches.

REVERSE THE ANGLED RIB PATTERN

NEXT ROW (RS): K1, slip the marker, work the established decrease (ssp or k2tog), work to the first center marker, yarn over, slip the marker, work to the second center marker, yarn over, slip the marker, work to the last 3 stitches, work the established decrease (p2tog or ssk), k1.

Continue working the Reverse Angled Rib Pattern, working yarn overs *after* the first center marker and *before* the second center marker on right-side rows and working new stitches into the pattern on wrong-side rows, *and at the same time,* when the piece measures approximately 23 (23, 23½, 23½, 24½, 24½)"/[58.5 (58.5, 59.5, 59.5, 62, 62)cm] from the beginning, shape the back neck as follows:

SHAPE NECK
Work the Reverse Angled Rib Pattern across 35 (35, 35, 35, 43, 43) stitches; join a second ball of yarn and bind off the middle 54 stitches, work in pattern to the end of the row.

Working both sides at once with separate balls of yarn, decrease 1 stitch at each neck edge once—34 (34, 34, 34, 42, 42) stitches remain each side.

Continue even in pattern until the piece measures approximately 24 (24, 24½, 24½, 25½, 25½)"/[61 (61, 62, 62, 65, 65)cm] from the beginning, ending after a wrong-side row.

Bind off in pattern.

Front

Work the same as the Back until the piece measures approximately 21 (21, 21½, 21½, 22½, 22½)"/[53.5 (53.5, 54.5, 54.5, 57, 57)cm] from the beginning, ending after a wrong-side row.

SHAPE NECK
NEXT ROW (RS): Work the Reverse Angled Rib Pattern across 49 (49, 49, 49, 57, 57) stitches; join a second ball of yarn and bind off the middle 26 stitches, work in pattern to the end of the row.

Working both sides at once with separate balls of yarn, bind off 4 stitches at each neck edge once; bind off 3 stitches each neck edge twice; bind off 2 sts each neck edge once, then decrease 1 stitch at each neck edge (working a k2tog at right neck edge and an ssk at left neck edge) every other row 3 times—34 (34, 34, 34, 42, 42) stitches remain each side.

Complete same as the Back.

Sleeves *(Make 2)*

With the larger needles, cast on 70 (70, 78, 78, 86, 86) stitches.

Begin the Rib Pattern, and work even until the piece measures approximately 1"/[2.5cm] from the beginning, ending after a wrong-side row.

Work fully fashioned increases (see Notes) each side every other row 15 (18, 20, 24, 24, 28) times, then every 4 rows 17 (14, 12, 8, 8, 4) times, working new stitches into the pattern as they accumulate—134 (134, 142, 142, 150, 150) stitches.

Continue even until the piece measures approximately 14 (14, 14½, 14½, 14½, 14½)"/[35.5 (35.5, 37, 37, 37, 37)cm] from the beginning or to the desired sleeve length to the shoulder, ending after a wrong-side row.

Bind off in pattern.

Finishing

Darn in all remaining yarn tails (page 156).

Block all pieces to the finished measurements (page 156).

Sew the right shoulder seam.

NECKBAND

With the right side facing, beginning at the left shoulder, and using the smaller needles, pick up and knit 158 stitches evenly spaced along the neckline.

Begin the Rib Pattern, matching the Rib Pattern as established in the garment; work even until the neckband measures approximately 1"/[2.5cm] from the beginning.

Bind off in pattern.

Sew the left shoulder seam, including the side of the neckband.

Set in the sleeves.

Sew the side and sleeve seams.

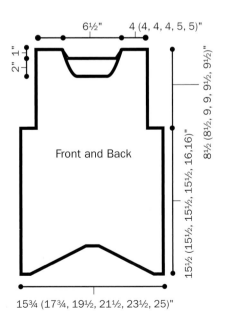

6½"   4 (4, 4, 4, 5, 5)"

2" 1"

8½ (8½, 9, 9, 9½, 9½)"

Front and Back

15½ (15½, 15½, 15½, 16,16)"

15¾ (17¾, 19½, 21½, 23½, 25)"

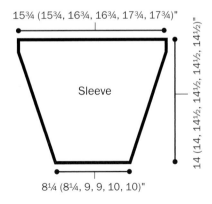

15¾ (15¾, 16¾, 16¾, 17¾, 17¾)"

Sleeve

14 (14, 14½, 14½, 14½, 14½)"

8¼ (8¼, 9, 9, 10, 10)"

Charlie

Use fully fashioned increases and decreases to take simple stripes to a totally new level! Instead of drawing attention to the widest part of the body, these angled stripes are actually quite flattering and are great fun to knit. Save the task of weaving in the ends for a mindless television project—or weave them in as you go (page 156).

Skill Level
Intermediate

Sizes
Small (Medium, Large, 1X, 2X, 3X, 4X). Instructions are for the smallest size, with changes for other sizes noted in parentheses as necessary.

Finished Measurements
Bust: 35 (39, 43, 47, 51, 55, 59)"/[89 (99, 109, 119.5, 129.5, 139.5, 150)cm]
Length: 20¼ (20¾, 21¼, 21¾, 21¾, 22¼, 22¼)"/[51.5 (52.5, 54, 55, 55, 56.5, 56.5)cm]

Materials
- Brown Sheep Company's *Naturespun Worsted* (4-medium/worsted weight; 100% wool; each approximately 3½ oz/[100g] and 245 yds/[224m]): 2 (2, 3, 3, 3, 4, 4) balls of Scarlet #N48 (A), 1 ball *each* of Peruvian Pink #N85 (B), Bougainvillea #105 (C), Salmon #145 (D), Mountain Purple #N80 (E), and Victorian Pink #N87 (F)  Medium
- Size 6 (4mm) knitting needles
- Size 7 (4.5mm) knitting needles or size needed to obtain gauge
- 3 stitch markers, 1 of them removable for the center stitch
- Blunt-end yarn needle

Gauge
20 stitches and 28 rows = 4"/[10cm] in stockinette stitch with the larger needles.
To save time, take time to check gauge.

Stitch Patterns
Stockinette Stitch (*any number of stitches*)
ROW 1 (RS): Knit across.
ROW 2: Purl across.
Repeat Rows 1 and 2 for the pattern.

Stripe Pattern (*22 rows*)

ROW 1 (RS): With B, knit across.

ROW 2: With C, purl across.

ROW 3: With C, knit across.

ROW 4: With B, purl across.

ROW 5: With D, knit across.

ROW 6: With D, purl across.

ROWS 7 AND 8: With E, purl across.

ROW 9: With F, knit across.

ROWS 10 AND 11: With A, same as Rows 2 and 3.

ROW 12: With F, purl across.

ROWS 13 AND 14: With B, same as Rows 5 and 6.

ROWS 15 AND 16: With D, same as Rows 7 and 8.

ROW 17: With E, same as Row 1.

ROWS 18 AND 19: With A, same as Rows 2 and 3.

ROW 20: With E, same as Row 4.

ROWS 21 AND 22: With F, same as Rows 7 and 8.

Repeat Rows 1–22 for the pattern.

Special Abbreviation

S2kp2 = Centered double decrease = Slip next 2 stitches at once knitwise, knit the next stitch, pass the 2 slipped stitches over the knit stitch.

Notes

- When working the M1 increases on the Front and Back, make them knitwise (page 151) or purlwise (page 152), depending on which row of the Stripe Pattern you are on.
- For fully fashioned increases: On knit rows, work 2 stitches in pattern, M1-R (page 15), work to the last 2 stitches, M1-L (page 14), work the last 2 stitches in pattern; on purled rows, work 2 stitches in pattern, M1 purlwise, work to the last 2 stitches, M1 purlwise, work the last 2 stitches in pattern.
- For fully fashioned decreases: On knit rows, work 2 stitches in pattern, ssk, work in pattern to the last 4 stitches, k2tog, work the last 2 stitches in pattern; on purled rows, p2, p2tog, work in pattern to the last 4 stitches, ssp, p2.
- For sweater assembly, refer to the illustration for set-in construction on page 158.

Back

With the smaller needles and A, cast on 81 (91, 101, 111, 121, 131, 141) stitches. Place a removable marker in the center stitch.

ROW 1 (RS): K17 (22, 27, 32, 37, 42, 47), place a marker, M1-R (see Notes), knit to 1 stitch before

the marked center stitch, s2kp2, k22, M1-L, place a marker, k17 (22, 27, 32, 37, 42, 47).

ROW 2: Knit across.

ROWS 3–6: Repeat Rows 1 and 2 twice more.

ROW 7 (RS) (CHEVRON ROW): Change to the larger needles and B, and begin the Stripe Pattern; work to the first marker, slip the marker, M1-R, work to 1 stitch before the marked center stitch, s2kp2, work to the next marker, M1-L, slip the marker, work to the end of the row.

Continuing the Stripe Pattern, repeat the Chevron Row every right-side row, *and at the same time,* work fully fashioned increases (see Notes) each side every 18 rows 4 times—89 (99, 109, 119, 129, 139, 149) stitches.

Continue even until the piece measures approximately 12¾"/[32.5cm] from the beginning, ending after a wrong-side row. *Make a note of which row of the Stripe Pattern you are on.*

SHAPE ARMHOLES

Continuing the established patterns, bind off 5 (6, 7, 7, 8, 8, 9) stitches at the beginning of the next 2 rows; bind off 2 (2, 3, 3, 4, 4, 5) stitches at the beginning of the next 2 rows; work fully fashioned decreases (see Notes) each side every row 0 (0, 0, 6, 8, 14, 17) times, every other row 0 (3, 6, 4, 3, 1, 0) times, then every 4 rows 2 (1, 0, 0, 0, 0, 0) times—71 (75, 77, 79, 83, 85, 87) stitches remain.

Continue even until the piece measures approximately 19¼ (19¾, 20¼, 20¾, 20¾, 21¼, 21¼)"/[49 (50, 51.5, 52.5, 52.5, 54, 54)cm] from the beginning, ending after a wrong-side row.

SHAPE NECK

Work 12 (14, 15, 16, 18, 19, 20) stitches in pattern, join a second ball of yarn and bind off the middle 47 stitches, work in pattern to the end of the row.

Working both sides at once with separate balls of yarn, work even until the piece measures approximately 20¼ (20¾, 21¼, 21¾, 21¾, 22¼, 22¼)"/[51.5 (52.5, 54, 55, 55, 56.5, 56.5)cm] from the beginning, ending both sides after the same wrong-side row.

Bind off in pattern.

Front

Work same as the Back.

Sleeves (Make 2)

With the smaller needles and A, cast on 40 (42, 42, 47, 47, 50, 54) stitches.

Knit 6 rows, and increase 7 (7, 7, 8, 8, 9, 9) stitches evenly across the last row using the M1 technique (page 14)—47 (49, 49, 55, 55, 59, 63) stitches.

Change to the larger needles and B, beginning the Stripe Pattern; work fully fashioned increases (see Notes) each side every 4 rows 0 (0, 0, 0, 0, 1, 4) times, every 6 rows 0 (0, 6, 6, 6, 12, 10) times, every 8 rows 0 (2, 5, 5, 5, 0, 0) times, every 10 rows 4 (6, 0, 0, 0, 0, 0) times, then every 12 rows 3 (0, 0, 0, 0, 0, 0) times—61 (65, 71, 77, 77, 85, 91) stitches.

Continue even until the piece measures approximately 12¾"/[32.5cm] from the beginning, ending after the same Stripe Pattern row that the Front and Back ended with just before the armhole shaping.

SHAPE CAP

Continuing the established patterns, bind off 5 (6, 7, 7, 8, 8, 9) stitches at the beginning of the next 2 rows,

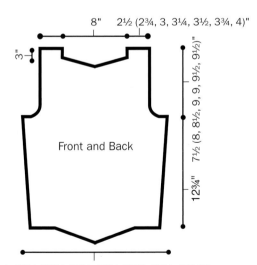

8" 2½ (2¾, 3, 3¼, 3½, 3¾, 4)"

3"

7½ (8, 8½, 9, 9, 9½, 9½)"

Front and Back

12¾"

Bust: 17½ (19½, 21½, 23½, 25½, 27½, 29½)"

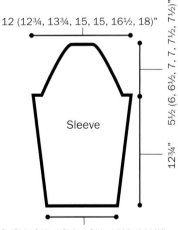

12 (12¾, 13¾, 15, 15, 16½, 18)"

5½ (6, 6½, 7, 7, 7½, 7½)"

Sleeve

12¾"

9 (9½, 9½, 10½, 10½, 11½, 11½)"

then work fully fashioned decreases (see Notes) each side every 4 rows 2 (2, 2, 1, 2, 0, 0) times, every other row 12 (13, 15, 19, 17, 23, 21) times, then every row 0 (0, 0, 0, 0, 0, 4) times—23 stitches remain.

Work 0 (1, 1, 0, 0, 0, 0) row even.

Bind off 2 stitches at the beginning of the next 4 rows—15 stitches remain.

Bind off.

Finishing

Darn in all remaining yarn tails (page 156).

Block all pieces to the finished measurements (page 156).

Sew the left shoulder seam.

NECKBAND

With the right side facing and using the smaller needles and A, pick up and knit 104 stitches evenly along the neckline. Place a marker on the center stitch on both the Front and the Back.

ROW 1 (WS): Knit to 2 stitches before the first marked stitch, s2kp2, knit to 2 stitches before the second marked stitch, s2kp2, knit to the end of the row—100 stitches remain.

ROW 2: Purl across.

ROW 3: Repeat Row 1, *and at the same time,* bind off.

Sew the right shoulder seam and neckband seam.

Set in the sleeves.

Sew the side and sleeve seams.

Jen

Here's the perfect feminine shell knit out of incredibly soft and luxurious cashmere yarn. Customize its fit with bust darts that match your bra cup size as described on page 131.

Skill Level
Experienced

Sizes
Extra Small (Small, Medium, Large, 1X, 2X, 3X, 4X). Instructions are for the smallest size, with changes for other sizes noted in parentheses as necessary.

Finished Measurements
Bust: 28 (30, 33, 36, 39, 42, 45, 48)"/ [71 (76, 84, 91, 99, 106.5, 114, 122)cm]
Length: 22 (22, 22½, 22½, 23, 23, 23½, 23½)"/[56 (56, 57, 57, 58.5, 58.5, 59.5, 59.5)cm]

Materials
- Jade Sapphire's *4-Ply Mongolian Cashmere* (3-light/DK weight; 100% cashmere; each approximately 2 oz/[55g] and 200yds/[183m]): 4 (4, 4, 5, 5, 5, 6, 6) hanks of Rose Quartz #33  Light
  Note: Larger cup sizes will require slightly more yarn.
- Size 3 (3.25mm) knitting needles, or size needed to obtain gauge
- Size 4 (3.5mm) knitting needles, or size needed to obtain gauge
- 5 stitch markers, 1 in a different color to mark the neck
- 2 stitch holders
- Blunt-end yarn needle

Gauge
26 stitches and 32 rows = 4"/[10cm] in the Cabled Rib Pattern with the larger needles;
24 stitches and 32 rows = 4"/[10cm] in stockinette stitch with the smaller needles.
To save time, take time to check gauge.

Stitch Patterns
Cabled Rib Pattern (*multiple of 4 + 2 stitches*)
ROW 1 (RS): P2, *Left Twist, p2; repeat from the * across.
ROW 2: K2, *Right Twist, k2; repeat from the * across.
Repeat Rows 1 and 2 for the pattern.
Or see the chart on page 132.

Fit
Very close-fitting

Figure Flattery

This wardrobe pleaser is a complete win-win: Its design details will make you look good and the luxurious cashmere yarn will make you feel good, too! Dozens of rickrack lines draw the eye up to the fitted empire waist, and custom-shaped bust darts will flaunt whatever you've got! If you don't dare to bare your upper arms, make simple short sleeves by picking up stitches along the armholes and work down a few inches.

Stockinette Stitch (*any number of stitches*)
ROW 1 (RS): Knit.
ROW 2: Purl
Repeat Rows 1 and 2 for the pattern.

Special Techniques

LEFT TWIST (RS): Skip the next stitch, then knit the following stitch *in its back loop;* knit the skipped stitch; slip both stitches off the left-hand needle together.

RIGHT TWIST (WS): Skip the next stitch, then *working in front of the skipped stitch,* purl the following stitch; purl the skipped stitch; slip both stitches off the left-hand needle together.

Notes

- For a perfect close fit, this sweater is designed with negative ease. The ribbed pattern will allow the fabric to stretch to fit the body, so knit the size you would normally knit for yourself.
- The instructions include bust shaping for a B-cup top; for other cup sizes, refer to the chart on page 131.
- The instructions include one selvedge stitch on each side; these stitches are not included in the finished measurements.
- For fully fashioned armhole decreases: On right-side rows, Left Twist, p2, ssk, work in pattern to the last 6 stitches, k2tog, p2, Left Twist; on wrong-side rows, Right Twist, k2, p2tog, work in pattern to the last 6 stitches, ssp, k2, Right Twist.
- For fully fashioned bust increases: *Work in pattern to the next marker, M1-R, slip the marker, k2, slip the marker, M1-L; repeat from the * once more, then work in pattern to the end of the row.
- For fully fashioned bust decreases: *Work in pattern to 2 stitches before the next marker, ssk, slip the marker, k2, slip the marker, k2tog; repeat from the * once more, then work in pattern to the end of the row.

Back

EMPIRE WAISTBAND

With the larger needles, cast on 10 stitches. Begin the Cabled Rib Pattern, and work even until the piece measures approximately 14 (15, 16½, 18, 19½, 21, 22½, 24)"/[35.5 (38, 42, 45.5, 49.5, 53.5, 57, 61) cm] from the beginning, ending after a right-side row.

Bind off in pattern.

LOWER BODY

With the right side facing and using the larger needles, pick up and knit 90 (98, 110, 118, 126, 138, 146, 158) stitches along one long edge of the Empire Waistband.

Beginning with Row 2 of the pattern, begin the Cabled Rib Pattern and work even until the Lower Body measures approximately 9¾"/[25cm] from the beginning, ending after a wrong-side row.

Bind off in pattern.

UPPER BODY

With the right side facing and using the smaller needles, pick up and knit 84 (90, 102, 110, 118, 126, 138, 146) stitches along the other long edge of the Empire Waistband.

Begin stockinette stitch, and work even until the piece measures approximately 15"/[38cm] from the bound-off edge of the Lower Body, ending after a wrong-side row.

SHAPE ARMHOLES

Bind off 6 (6, 12, 12, 18, 18, 24, 24) stitches at the beginning of the next 2 rows, then keeping first and last 4 stitches each side in the Cable Rib Pattern throughout, work fully fashioned armhole decreases (see Notes) every row 0 (2, 0, 0, 0, 0, 0, 0) times, every other row 0 (0, 0, 4, 0, 3, 0, 6) times, every 4 rows 2 (2, 3, 4, 2, 5, 7, 4) times, then every 6 rows 2 (2, 2, 0, 3, 0, 0, 0) times—64 (66, 68, 70, 72, 74, 76, 78) stitches remain.

Continue even in pattern until the piece measures approximately 21 (21, 21½, 21½, 22, 22, 22½, 22½)"/[53.5 (53.5, 54.5, 54.5, 56, 56, 57, 57)cm] from the beginning, ending after a wrong-side row.

SHAPE NECK

Work 11 (12, 13, 14, 15, 16, 17, 18) stitches in pattern, join a second ball of yarn and bind off the middle 42 stitches, work in pattern to the end of the row.

Work even on both sides at once with separate balls of yarn until the piece measures approximately 22 (22, 22½, 22½, 23, 23, 23½, 23½)"/56 (56, 57, 57, 58.5, 58.5, 59.5, 59.5)cm] from the beginning, ending after a wrong-side row.

Bind off in pattern.

Front

Work same as the Back until the Upper Body measures approximately 10¾"/[27.5cm] from bound-off edge of the Lower Body, ending after a right-side row. Note: Instructions are for B cup. Other cup sizes begin their bust shaping at a different point; check the chart opposite.

NEXT ROW (WS): P24 (26, 29, 31, 34, 36, 37, 40), place a marker, p2, place a marker, p32 (34, 40, 44, 46, 50, 60, 62), place a marker, p2, place a marker, p24 (26, 29, 31, 34, 36, 37, 40).

SHAPE BUST

For B cup, work fully fashioned bust increases (see Notes) every 4 rows 6 times; *for all sizes,* work 4 rows even; *for B cup,* work fully fashioned bust decreases (see Notes) every 4 rows 4 times, then every other row twice, *and at the same time,* when the piece measures approximately 15"/[38cm] from the bound-off edge of the Lower Body, ending after a wrong-side row, shape

the armholes same as for the Back, *and at the same time,* shape the neck as follows.

SHAPE NECK

Place a different-colored marker between the 2 middle stitches.

ROW 1 (RS): Continuing the bust shaping as established and beginning the armhole shaping, work in pattern to 6 stitches before the center marker, k2tog, p2, Left Twist; join a second ball of yarn, Left Twist, p2, ssk, work to the end of the row.

ROW 2: Continuing the bust and armhole shapings, work in pattern to 6 stitches before the center marker, ssp, k2, Right Twist; with the second ball of yarn, Right Twist, k2, p2tog, work to the end of the row.

Continuing the bust and armhole shapings, work fully fashioned neck decreases and Left/Right Twists as established on next row, then every other row 7 more times, then every 4 rows 7 times—15 (16, 17, 18, 19, 20, 21, 22) stitches remain each side when all shaping is complete.

Continue even until the piece measures approximately 22 (22, 22½, 22½, 23, 23, 23½, 23½)"/[56 (56, 57, 57, 58.5, 58.5, 59.5, 59.5)cm] from the beginning, ending after a wrong-side row.

Bind off 11 (12, 13, 14, 15, 16, 17, 18) stitches at the beginning of the next 2 rows—4 stitches remain each side. Put these stitches on holders.

Finishing

Darn in all remaining yarn tails (page 156).

Block all pieces to the finished measurements (page 156).

Sew the shoulder seams.

NECKBANDS
Transfer the 4 stitches on each side of the Front neck to a knitting needle. Continue even until the straps, *when slightly stretched,* meet at the center back of the neck.

Bind off.

Sew the sides of the neckbands to the back neckline.

Sew the bound-off edges of the neckbands together at the back of the neck.

Sew the side seams.

Different Bra Cup Sizes

Note: The B-cup size is given in the written pattern.

CUP SIZE	Length at Which to Begin Shaping Bust Darts	Amount of Fabric Added for Cup Size	Increase Rate	Decrease Rate
AA	10¾"/[27.5cm]	½"/[1.5cm] = 2 stitches = 1 increase/decrease	Every 20 rows once	Every 16 rows once
A	10¾"/[27.5cm]	1"/[2.5cm] = 6 stitches = 3 increases/decreases	Every 8 rows 3 times	Every 8 rows once, then every 6 rows twice
B	10¾"/[27.5cm]	2"/[5cm] = 12 stitches = 6 increases/decreases	Every 4 rows 6 times	Every 4 rows 4 times, then every other row twice
C	10¾"/[27.5cm]	3"/[7.5cm] = 18 stitches = 9 increases/decreases	Every other row 6 times, then every 4 rows 3 times	Every 4 rows once, then every other row 8 times
D	10½"/[26.5cm]	4"/[10cm] = 24 stitches = 12 increases/decreases	Every other row 8 times, then every 4 rows 4 times	Every other row 12 times
DD or E	10¼"/[26cm]	5"/[12.5cm] = 30 stitches = 15 increases/decreases	Every other row 12 times, then every 4 rows 3 times	Every 4 rows once then every other row 14 times

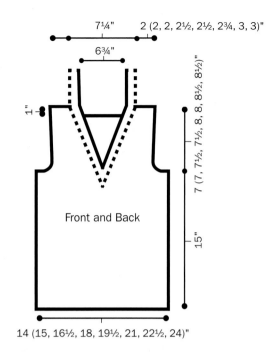

7¼"   2 (2, 2, 2½, 2½, 2¾, 3, 3)"

6¾"

7 (7, 7½, 7½, 8, 8, 8½, 8½)"

1"

Front and Back

15"

14 (15, 16½, 18, 19½, 21, 22½, 24)"

CABLED RIB PATTERN

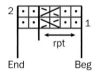

2

1

rpt

End   Beg

Stitch Key

□ = K on RS; p on WS

• = P on RS; k on WS

⤬ = Left Twist = Slip next st onto cn and hold in front; k1; k1 from cn; **OR** skip first st and knit next st *in back loop*; then knit the skipped st; slip both sts off left-hand needle together

⤬ = Right Twist on WS = Skip the first stitch, then working in front of the skipped stitch, purl the next st, purl the skipped stitch, then slip both stitches off the left-hand needle together

Sydney

Light as air, this mohair and silk tunic is a perfect transitional piece for autumn or spring. It's knit in the round until the armholes and has a beautiful incorporated neck treatment.

Skill Level
Experienced

Sizes
Small (Medium, Large, 1X, 2X, 3X, 4X). Instructions are for the smallest size, with changes for the other sizes noted in parentheses as necessary.

Finished Measurements
Bust: 31½ (35, 38¾, 42½, 46, 50, 53½)"/[80 (89, 98.5, 108, 117, 127, 136)cm]
Hip: 55½ (59, 62¾, 66½, 70, 74, 77½)"/[141 (150, 159.5, 169, 178, 188, 197)cm]
Length (*at center front*): 28 (28½, 29, 29½, 29½, 30, 30)"/[71 (72, 74, 75, 75, 76, 76)cm]

Materials
• Westminster Fibers/Rowan's *Kidsilk Haze* (2-fine/sport weight; 70% super kid mohair/30% silk; each approximately 1 oz/[25g] and 229 yds/ [210m]): 7 (8, 9, 10, 11, 12, 13) balls of Dewberry #600  Fine
• Size 2 (2.75mm) 29"/[74cm] circular needle
• Size 3 (3.25mm) 29"/[74cm] circular needle or size needed to obtain gauge
• 8 stitch markers (1 in a different color than the others to mark the beginning of rounds)
• Waste yarn to hold stitches
• Blunt-end yarn needle

Gauge
26 stitches and 38 rounds/rows = 4"/[10cm] in stockinette stitch with the larger needle.
To save time, take time to check gauge.

Stitch Patterns
Garter Stitch (*in the round; any number of stitches*)
ROUND 1 (RS): Knit.
ROUND 2: Purl.
Repeat Rounds 1 and 2 for the pattern.

Garter Stitch (*worked flat; any number of stitches*)
ROW 1 (RS): Knit.
PATTERN ROW: As Row 1.

Fit
Close-fitting

Figure Flattery

With its A-line silhouette and rows of eyelets pointing upward, this design is universally flattering. The neckline is even framed with delicate eyelets!

Stockinette Stitch (*worked flat; any number of stitches*)

ROW 1 (RS): Knit.

ROW 2: Purl.

Repeat Rows 1 and 2 for the pattern.

Notes

- The Body of this sweater is worked in the round from the bottom up to the armholes and then is divided, after which the Front and Back are worked flat. The sleeves are worked flat.
- For fully fashioned armhole decreases: On right-side rows, k2, sssk, work in pattern to the last 5 stitches, k3tog, k2; on wrong-side rows, p2, p2tog, purl to the last 4 stitches, ssp, p2.
- On the right-hand side of the neck, k2, ssk, knit to 7 stitches before the neck edge, k2tog, yarn over, p5; on the left-hand side of the neck, p5, yarn over, ssk, knit to the last 4 stitches, k2tog, k2. On the subsequent row, purl across all stitches.
- For fully fashioned sleeve cap decreases: On right-side rows, k2, ssk, knit to the last 4 stitches, k2tog, k2; on wrong-side rows, p2, p2tog, purl to the last 4 stitches, ssp, p2.
- For sweater assembly, refer to the illustration for set-in construction on page 158.

Body

With the smaller needle, cast on 317 (338, 359, 380, 401, 422, 444) stitches. Place a marker for the beginning of the round and join, being careful not to twist the stitches.

Begin garter stitch in the round, and work even until the piece measures approximately ½"/[1.5cm] from the beginning, ending after a knit round.

NEXT ROUND: Purl around, and use the M1 purlwise technique (page 15) to increase 43 (46, 49, 52, 55, 58, 60) stitches evenly spaced—360 (384, 408, 432, 456, 480, 504) stitches.

SET UP PATTERN

NEXT ROUND: Change to the larger needle; *k2, ssk, k71 (77, 83, 89, 95, 101, 107), yarn over, place a marker, k30, place a marker, yarn over, k71 (77, 83, 89, 95, 101, 107), k2tog, k2**; place a marker; repeat from the * to the ** once more.

MAIN PATTERN ROUND 1: Knit around.

MAIN PATTERN ROUND 2: *K2, ssk, knit to the next marker, yarn over, slip the marker, k30, slip the marker, yarn over, knit to 4 stitches before the next marker, k2tog, k2; repeat from the * once more.

MAIN PATTERN ROUND 3: Knit around.

MAIN PATTERN ROUND 4 (DECREASE ROUND): *K2, sssk, knit to the next marker, yarn over, slip the marker, k30, slip the marker, yarn over, knit to 5 stitches before the next marker, k3tog, k2; repeat from the * once more—356 (380, 404, 428, 452, 476, 500) stitches remain.

Repeat the last 4 rounds 38 more times, with each set of 4 rounds having 4 fewer stitches than the previous 4 rounds—204 (228, 252, 276, 300, 324, 348) stitches remain.

Repeat Main Pattern Rounds 1 and 2 *only* until the piece measures approximately 20"/[51cm] from the beginning, measured at the center front, ending with Main Pattern Round 1, and 4 (6, 8, 10, 12, 14, 16) stitches before the beginning of the round marker.

SHAPE ARMHOLES

Removing the beginning of round marker, *bind off the next 8 (12, 16, 20, 24, 28, 32) stitches, k2, ssk, knit to the next marker, yarn over, slip the marker, k30, slip the marker, yarn over**, knit to 8 (10, 12, 14, 16, 18, 20) stitches before the next marker, k2tog, k2; join a second ball of yarn and repeat from * to ** once more, then knit to the last 4 stitches, k2tog, k2. Slip the last 94 (102, 110, 118, 126, 134, 142) stitches onto waste yarn to hold for the Front.

BACK ARMHOLE SHAPING

ROW 1 (WS): Bind off 2 (2, 4, 4, 6, 6, 8), purl to the end of the row—92 (100, 106, 114, 120, 128, 134) stitches remain.

ROW 2: Bind off 2 (2, 4, 4, 6, 6, 8), k2 (including the stitch on right-hand needle from the bind-off), ssk, knit to the next marker, yarn over, slip the marker, k30, slip the marker, yarn over, knit to the last 4 stitches, k2tog, k2—90 (98, 102, 110, 114, 122, 126) stitches remain.

Continuing in the established pattern, work fully fashioned armhole decreases (see Notes) each side every row 0 (1, 1, 1, 1, 3, 3) times, every other row 1 (2, 1, 4, 4, 4, 4) times, then every 4 rows 2 (2, 3, 2, 2, 2, 2) times—84 (88, 92, 96, 100, 104, 108) stitches remain.

Continue even in pattern (on right-side rows, working the decreases 2 stitches in from each side with the yarn overs on each side of the marked center stitches) until the piece measures approximately 24 (24½, 25, 25½, 26, 26, 26½, 26½)"/[61 (62, 63.5, 65, 66, 66, 67.5, 67.5)cm] from the beginning, ending after a wrong-side row.

NEXT ROW (RS): K2, ssk, knit to the first marker, yarn over, slip the marker, p30, slip the marker, yarn over, knit to the last 4 stitches, k2tog, k2.

NEXT ROW: Purl to the first marker, slip the marker, p30, slip the marker, purl to the end of the row.

Repeat the last 2 rows 4 more times.

SHAPE NECK

ROW 1 (RS): K2, ssk, knit to 2 stitches before the marker, k2tog, yarn over, slip the marker, p5; join a second ball of yarn and bind off the middle 20 stitches purlwise; p5, slip the marker, yarn over, ssk, knit to the last 4 stitches, k2tog, k2—31 (33, 35, 37, 39, 41, 43) stitches remain each side.

ROW 2: Working both sides at once with separate balls of yarn, purl across both sides.

Work fully fashioned neck decreases (see Notes) each side every other row 12 more times, ending after a wrong-side row—19 (21, 23, 25, 27, 29, 31) stitches remain each side.

SHAPE SHOULDERS

ROW 1 (RS): Bind off 4 (4, 5, 5, 6, 7, 7) stitches, knit to 2 stitches before the marker, k2tog, yarn over, slip the marker, p5; p5, slip the marker, yarn over, ssk, knit to the end of the row.

ROW 2: Bind off 4 (4, 5, 5, 6, 7, 7) stitches, purl across both sides—15 (17, 18, 20, 21, 22, 24) stitches remain each side.

Repeat the last 2 rows twice more (eliminating the yarn over and decrease when there are no longer enough stitches to work them), then bind off 7 (9, 8, 10, 9, 8, 10) stitches at the beginning of the next 2 rows.

FRONT ARMHOLE SHAPING

Slip the 94 (102, 110, 118, 126, 134, 142) Front stitches from the waste yarn to the larger needle.

ROW 1 (WS): Bind off 2 (2, 4, 4, 6, 6, 8), purl to the end of the row—92 (100, 106, 114, 120, 128, 134) stitches remain.

ROW 2: Bind off 2 (2, 4, 4, 6, 6, 8) sts, k2 (including the stitch on right-hand needle from the bind-off), ssk, knit to the next marker, yarn over, slip the marker, k30, slip the marker, yarn over, knit to the last 4 stitches, k2tog, k2—90 (98, 102, 110, 114, 122, 126) stitches remain.

Continuing in pattern, work fully fashioned armhole decreases (see Notes) each side every row 0 (1, 1, 1, 1, 3, 3) times, every other row 1 (2, 1, 4, 4, 4, 4) times, then every 4 rows 2 (2, 3, 2, 2, 2, 2) times, *and at the same time,* when the piece measures approximately 20½ (21, 21½, 22, 22, 22½, 22½)"/[52 (53.5, 54.5, 56, 56, 57, 57)cm] from the beginning, ending after a wrong-side row, work as follows:

NEXT ROW (RS): Continuing armhole shaping as necessary, work to the first marker, yarn over, slip the marker, p30, slip the marker, yarn over, work to the end of the row.

NEXT ROW: Continuing armhole shaping as necessary, purl across.

Repeat the last 2 rows 4 more times.

SHAPE NECK

ROW 1 (RS): K2, ssk, knit to 2 sts before the marker, k2tog, yarn over, slip the marker, p5; join a second ball of yarn and bind off the middle 20 stitches, p5, slip the marker, yarn over, ssk, knit to the last 4 stitches, k2tog, k2—31 (33, 35, 37, 39, 41, 43) stitches remain each side.

ROW 2: Working both sides at once with separate balls of yarn, purl across both sides.

Work fully fashioned neck decreases (see Notes) each side every 4 rows 12 more times, ending after a wrong-side row—19 (21, 23, 25, 27, 29, 31) stitches remain each side.

SHAPE SHOULDERS
Work as for the Back.

Sleeves *(Make 2)*
With the smaller needle, cast on 68 (68, 73, 81, 86, 91, 97) stitches. Do not join.

Begin garter stitch worked flat, and work even until the piece measures approximately ½"/[1.5cm] from the beginning, ending after a wrong-side row, and on the last row, use the M1 purlwise technique (page 15) to increase 10 (10, 11, 11, 12, 13, 13) stitches evenly spaced across the row—78 (78, 84, 92, 98, 104, 110) stitches.

Change to the larger needle and begin stockinette stitch; continue even until the piece measures approximately 4"/[10cm] from the beginning, ending after a wrong-side row.

SHAPE CAP
Bind off 4 (6, 8, 10, 12, 14, 16) stitches at the beginning of the next 2 rows, then work fully fashioned sleeve cap decreases each side every 4 rows 0 (0, 0, 1, 0, 2, 1) times, every other row 11 (13, 15, 13, 15, 11, 13) times, then every row 9 (5, 1, 0, 0, 0, 0) times—30 (30, 36, 44, 44, 50, 50) stitches remain.

Work 0 (0, 0, 1, 1, 1, 1) row even.

Bind off 3 stitches at the beginning of the next 4 rows—18 (18, 24, 32, 32, 38, 38) stitches remain.

Bind off.

Finishing
Block the pieces to the finished measurements (page 156).

Use mattress stitch (page 156) to sew the shoulder seams.

Set in the sleeves.

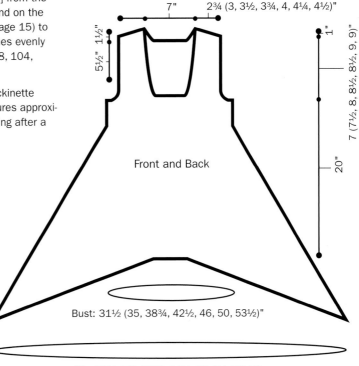

7" 2¾ (3, 3½, 3¾, 4, 4¼, 4½)"

5½" 1½"

1"

7 (7½, 8, 8½, 8½, 9, 9)"

Front and Back

20"

Bust: 31½ (35, 38¾, 42½, 46, 50, 53½)"

Hip: 55½ (59, 62¾, 66½, 70, 74, 77½)"

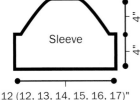

2¾ (2¾, 3¾, 5, 5, 5¾, 5¾)"

4"

4"

Sleeve

12 (12, 13, 14, 15, 16, 17)"

Trompe l'Oeil

Would you like to instantly shrink the size of your hips? This clever design uses diagonal lines to create the illusion of a tapered silhouette. Like other sweaters in this book, its integrated neckband makes it easy—and tons of fun!—to finish.

Skill Level
Intermediate

Sizes
Extra Small (Small, Medium, Large, 1X, 2X, 3X). Instructions are for the smallest size, with changes for other sizes noted in parentheses as necessary.

Finished Measurements
Bust: 33 (36, 39, 44, 47, 52, 57)"/[84 (91, 99, 112, 119.5, 132, 145)cm]
Length: 23 (23½, 23½, 24, 24, 24½, 24½)"/[58.5 (59.5, 59.5, 61, 61, 62, 62)cm]

Materials
- Zealana Yarns' *Willow DK* (3-light/DK weight; 70% merino wool/30% cashmere; each approximately 1¾ oz/[50g] and 140 yds/[128m]): 7 (8, 8, 9, 9, 10, 11) balls of Emerald #14  Light
- Size 6 (4mm) knitting needles or size needed to obtain gauge
- 5 stitch markers
- Blunt-end yarn needle

Gauge
24 stitches and 32 rows = 4"/[10cm] in Garter Rib Pattern.
To save time, take time to check gauge.

Stitch Patterns
Garter Rib Pattern (*multiple of 4 + 2 stitches*)
ROW 1 (RS): K2, *p2, k2; repeat from the * across.
ROW 2: Purl across.
Repeat Rows 1 and 2 for the pattern.

Diagonal Lines Pattern
Work in established Garter Rib, working new stitches into the pattern as they accumulate.
ROW 1 (RS): Work to 2 stitches before the first marker, k2tog, slip the marker, work to the next marker, slip the marker, M1-R (page 15), work to the next marker, M1-L, slip the marker, work to the next marker, slip the marker, ssk, work to the end of the row.

(pattern continues)

Fit
Standard-fitting

Figure Flattery

Oodles of vertical lines make this design especially flattering. Its two diagonal lines at the hip and an open V-neck make this one a winner for everyone's figure!

ROW 2 AND ALL WRONG-SIDE ROWS: Purl across.

ROW 3: Work in the established pattern.

ROW 5: As Row 1.

ROW 7: Work in the established pattern.

ROW 9: Work to 2 stitches before the first marker, k2tog, slip the marker, work to the next marker, slip the marker, M1 purlwise (page 15), work to the next marker, M1 purlwise, slip the marker, work to the next marker, slip the marker, ssk, work to the end of the row.

ROW 11: Work in the established pattern.

ROW 13: As Row 9.

ROW 15: Work in the established pattern.

ROW 16: As Row 2.

Repeat Rows 1–16 for the pattern.

Notes

- The instructions include one selvedge stitch on each side; these stitches are not included in the finished measurements.
- The stitch count will remain constant on every row until the armholes are shaped, after which it will remain constant until the beginning of the neck shaping.
- For fully fashioned armhole decreases: On right-side rows, [k2, p2] 3 times, k1, ssk, work in pattern to the last 15 stitches, k2tog, k1, [p2, k2] 3 times; on wrong-side rows, p13, p2tog, purl to the last 15 stitches, ssp, purl to the end of the row.
- For fully fashioned neck decreases: On the right-hand side of the neck, work to 16 stitches before the neck edge, k2tog, k1, [p2, k2] 3 times, k1; on the left-hand side of the neck, k1, [k2, p2] 3 times, k1, ssk, work to the end of the row.
- For fully fashioned sleeve increases: For the first 2 sets of increases, work to the first marker, M1-R, slip the marker, work to the next marker, slip the marker, M1-L, work to the end of the row; for the next 2 sets of increases, work to the first marker, M1 purlwise, slip the marker, work to the next marker, slip the marker, M1 purlwise, work to the end of the row.
- For fully fashioned sleeve cap decreases: On right-side rows, [k2, p2] 2 times, k1, ssk, work in pattern to the last 11 stitches, k2tog, k1, [p2, k2] 2 times; on wrong-side rows, p9, p2tog, purl to the last 11 stitches, ssp, purl to the end of the row.
- For sweater assembly, refer to the illustration for set-in construction on page 158.

Back

Cast on 102 (110, 118, 134, 142, 158, 174) stitches.

Begin the Garter Rib Pattern, and work even until the piece measures approximately 4"/[10cm] from the beginning, ending after a right-side row.

NEXT ROW (WS): P17 (21, 25, 33, 37, 45, 53) stitches, place a marker, p13, place a marker, p42, place a marker, p13, place a marker, purl to the end of the row.

BEGIN DIAGONAL LINES PATTERN

Work the 16-row Diagonal Lines Pattern 4 times for Extra Small and 5 times for all other sizes.

Continue even in Garter Rib, if necessary, until the piece measures approximately 15½"/[39.5cm] from the beginning, ending after a wrong-side row.

SHAPE ARMHOLES

Bind off 4 (4, 4, 8, 8, 12, 16) stitches at the beginning of the next 2 rows, then work fully fashioned armhole decreases (see Notes) every row 2 (8, 8, 14, 14, 12, 20) times, then every other row 6 (4, 4, 2, 2, 4, 0) times—78 (78, 86, 86, 94, 102, 102) stitches remain.

Continue even until the piece measures approximately 20½ (21, 21, 21½, 21½, 22, 22)"/[52 (53.5, 53.5, 54.5, 54.5, 56, 56)cm] from the beginning, ending after a wrong-side row.

SHAPE NECK

Work 5 (5, 9, 9, 13, 17, 17) stitches in pattern; join a second ball of yarn and bind off the middle 68 stitches, work in pattern to the end of the row.

Work a fully fashioned neck decrease (see Notes) at each neck edge on the next right-side row—4 (4, 8, 8, 12, 16, 16) stitches remain each side.

Continue even until the piece measures approximately 23 (23½, 23½, 24, 24, 24½, 24½)"/[58.5 (59.5, 59.5, 61, 61, 62, 62)cm] from the beginning, ending after a wrong-side row.

Bind off all stitches as they present themselves.

Front

Work same as the Back until the piece measures approximately 16 (16½, 16½, 17, 17, 17½, 17½)"/ [40.5 (42, 42, 43, 43, 44.5, 44.5)cm] from the beginning, ending after a wrong-side row.

Place a marker between the 2 center stitches for Front neck edge.

SHAPE NECK

Continue armhole decreases same as for the Back, *and at the same time,* work fully fashioned neck decreases (see Notes) every other row 16 times, then every 4 rows 4 times, joining a second ball of yarn at the center marker on the first row, then using separate balls of yarn for Left and Right Fronts thereafter—19 (19, 23, 23, 27, 31, 31) stitches remain each side.

Continue even until the piece measures the same as the Back to the shoulders.

Bind off 4 (4, 8, 8, 12, 16, 16) stitches at the beginning of the next 2 rows—15 stitches remain each side. Put these stitches on holders.

Sleeves *(Make 2)*

Cast on 62 (62, 70, 70, 78, 78, 78) stitches.

Begin the Garter Rib Pattern and work even for 18 (12, 12, 10, 12, 14, 14) rows; on the last row, place

markers after the first 12 stitches and before the last 12 stitches.

Work fully fashioned increases (see Notes) on the next row, then every other row 0 (0, 0, 0, 0, 7, 7) times, every 4 rows 0 (3, 0, 11, 11, 8, 8) times, every 6 rows 0 (4, 7, 0, 0, 0, 0) times, then every 10 rows 3 (0, 0, 0, 0, 0, 0) times—70 (78, 86, 94, 102, 110, 110) stitches.

Continue even until the piece measures approximately 7 (7, 7½, 7½, 8, 8, 8)"/[18 (18, 19, 19, 20.5, 20.5, 20.5)cm] from the beginning, or desired length to underarm, ending after a wrong-side row.

SHAPE CAP

Bind off 4 (4, 4, 8, 8, 12, 16) stitches at the beginning of the next 2 rows, then work fully fashioned sleeve cap decreases (see Notes) every right-side row 13 (13, 9, 13, 9, 13, 17) times, then every row 7 (11, 19, 15, 23, 19, 11) times—22 stitches remain.

Bind off 3 stitches at the beginning of the next 4 rows—10 stitches remain.

Bind off in the pattern.

Finishing

Darn in all remaining yarn tails (page 156).

Block all pieces to the finished measurements (page 156).

Sew the shoulder seams.

BACK NECKBAND

Transfer the 15 stitches of one neckband to one of the knitting needles. Continue in pattern until the band, *when slightly stretched,* reaches the center back of the neck. Bind off. Repeat on the other side.

Sew the sides of neckband to the back neckline.

Sew the bound-off edges of neckband together at the back of the neck.

Set in the sleeves.

Sew the side and sleeve seams.

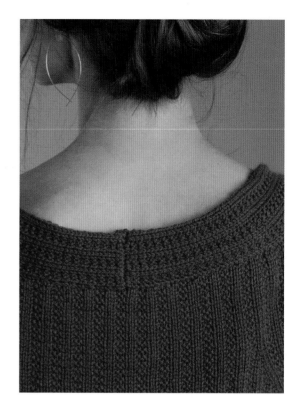

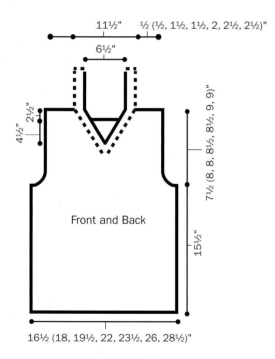

11½"   ½ (½, 1½, 1½, 2, 2½, 2½)"

6½"

2½"

4½"

7½ (8, 8, 8½, 8½, 9, 9)"

15½"

Front and Back

16½ (18, 19½, 22, 23½, 26, 28½)"

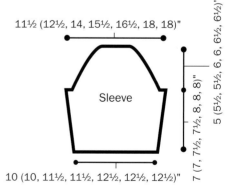

11½ (12½, 14, 15½, 16½, 18, 18)"

Sleeve

5 (5½, 5½, 6, 6, 6½, 6½)"

7 (7, 7½, 7½, 8, 8, 8)"

10 (10, 11½, 11½, 12½, 12½, 12½)"

Angie

Incorporated armholes and neck shaping make this design especially fun to knit—and easy to finish. It's ideal for hot-weather knitting!

Skill Level
Intermediate

Sizes
Small (Medium, Large, 1X, 2X, 3X). Instructions are for the smallest size, with changes for other sizes noted in parentheses as necessary.

Finished Measurements
Bust: 32 (36, 40, 44, 48, 52)"/ [81 (91, 101.5, 112, 122, 132)cm]
Lower Edge: 48 (54, 60, 66, 72, 78)"/[122 (137, 152.5, 167.5, 183, 198) cm]
Length: 29 (29½, 29½, 30, 30, 30½)"/[74 (75, 75, 76, 76, 77.5)cm]

Materials
- Louet North America's *Euroflax Fine* (2-fine/sport weight; 100% linen; each approximately 3½ oz/[100g] and 270 yds/247m]): 4 (5, 5, 6, 6, 7) hanks of Steel Grey #68 **2** Fine
- Size 2 (2.75mm) knitting needles
- Size 3 (3.25mm) knitting needles or size needed to obtain gauge
- 2 Size 2 (2.75mm) double-pointed needles
- Blunt-end yarn needle

Gauge
24 stitches and 32 rows = 4"/[10cm] with the larger needles in the Lace Pattern D after blocking.
To save time, take time to check gauge.

Stitch Patterns
Lace Pattern A (*multiple of 18 + 19 stitches*)
See chart.

Lace Pattern B (*multiple of 16 + 17 stitches*)
See chart.

Lace Pattern C (*multiple of 14 + 15 stitches*)
See chart.

Lace Pattern D (*multiple of 12 + 13 stitches*)
See chart.

Rib Pattern (*multiple of 4 + 1 stitches*)
ROW 1 (RS): K1, *p3, k1; repeat from the * across.
ROW 2: P1, *k3, p1; repeat from the * across.
Repeat Rows 1–2 for the pattern.

Special Abbreviations

S2kp2 = Centered double decrease = Slip next 2 stitches at once knitwise, knit the next stitch, pass the 2 slipped stitches over the knit stitch.

MB = Make a bobble = Knit into [front, back, front] of the next stitch, turn; p1, [p1, yarn over, p1] all into the same st, p1, turn; k5, turn; p2tog, p1, p2tog, turn; s2kp2.

Notes

- For fully fashioned armhole decreases: On right-side rows, [k1, p3] twice, ssk, work in pattern to the last 10 stitches, k2tog, [p3, k1] twice; on wrong-side rows, [p1, k3] twice, p2tog, work in pattern to the last 10 stitches, ssp, [k3, p1] twice.
- For fully fashioned neck decreases: On the right-hand side of the neck, work to the last 10 stitches before the neck edge, k2tog, [p3, k1] twice; on the left-hand side of the neck, [k1, p3] twice, ssk, work to the end of the row.

Back

With the smaller needles, cast on 145 (163, 181, 199, 217, 235) stitches.

BOBBLE ROW (WS): K18, *MB, k17; repeat from the * to the last stitch, k1.

NEXT ROW: Knit across.

Change to the larger needles; begin Lace Pattern A, and work Rows 1–32 once, then work Rows 1–6.

DECREASE ROW 1 (RS): P2tog, k7, p1, *k7, s2kp2, k7, p1; repeat from the * to the last 9 stitches, k7, ssp—129 (145, 161, 177, 193, 209) stitches remain.

NEXT ROW (WS): Knit the knit stitches and purl the purl stitches as you see them.

Begin Lace Pattern B, and work Rows 1–32 once, then work Rows 1–6.

DECREASE ROW 2 (RS): P2tog, k6, p1, *k6, s2kp2, k6, p1; repeat from the * to the last 8 stitches, k6, ssp—113 (127, 141, 155, 169, 183) stitches remain.

NEXT ROW (WS): Knit the knit stitches and purl the purl stitches as you see them.

Begin Lace Pattern C, and work Rows 1–32 once, then work Rows 1–6.

DECREASE ROW 3 (RS): P2tog, k5, p1, *k5, s2kp2,

k5, p1; repeat from the * to the last 7 stitches, k5, ssp—97 (109, 121, 133, 145, 157) stitches remain.

NEXT ROW (WS): Knit the knit stitches and purl the purl stitches as you see them.

Begin Lace Pattern D, and work Rows 1–26.

Continue in the Rib Pattern, and work even until the piece measures approximately 20¼"/[51.5cm] from the beginning, ending after a wrong-side row.

SHAPE ARMHOLES

Bind off 4 (4, 8, 8, 8, 12) stitches at the beginning of the next 2 rows, then work fully fashioned decreases (see Notes) each side every row 0 (2, 2, 12, 20, 18) times, every other row 4 (8, 8, 8, 4, 6) times, then every 4 rows 4 (2, 2, 0, 0, 0) times—73 (77, 81, 77, 81, 85) stitches remain.

Continue even until the piece measures approximately 27 (27½, 27½, 28, 28, 28½)"/[68.5 (70, 70, 71, 71, 72)cm] from the beginning, ending after a wrong-side row.

SHAPE NECK

Work 17 stitches in pattern, join a second ball of yarn and bind off the middle 39 (43, 47, 43, 47, 51) stitches in the pattern, work to the end of the row.

Work both sides at once with separate balls of yarn until the piece measures approximately 28 (28½, 28½, 29, 29, 29½)"/[71 (72, 72, 74, 74, 75)cm] from the beginning, ending after a wrong-side row.

SHAPE SHOULDERS

Bind off 4 stitches at the beginning of the next 6 rows, then bind off 5 stitches at the beginning of the next 2 rows.

Front

Work same as the Back until the piece measures approximately 23 (23½, 23½, 24, 24, 24½)"/[58.5 (59.5, 59.5, 61, 61, 62)cm] from the beginning, ending after a wrong-side row.

SHAPE NECK

Work 29 stitches in pattern, join a second ball of yarn and bind off the middle 15 (19, 23, 19, 23, 27) stitches in the pattern, work across to the end of the row.

Stitch Key

☐ = K on RS; p on WS

· = P on RS; k on WS

o = Yarn over

⟋ = K2tog

⟍ = Ssk

◢ = Ssp

⟍ = P2tog

▲ = Insert needle into the second and first sts as if to p2tog-through-back loops; slip these 2 sts onto the RH needle in this position; p1; p2sso

LACE PATTERN A

18-stitch repeat

End · · · Beg

LACE PATTERN B

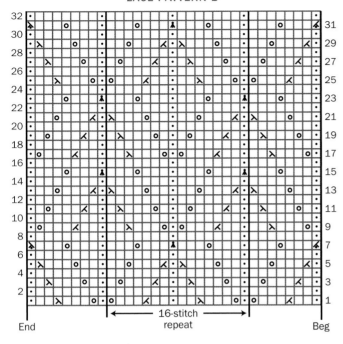

16-stitch repeat

End   Beg

LACE PATTERN C

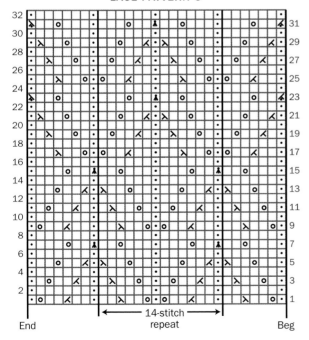

14-stitch repeat

End   Beg

LACE PATTERN D

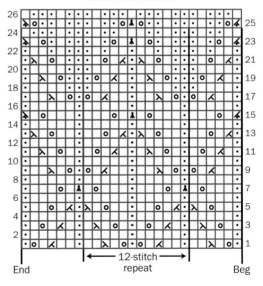

12-stitch repeat

End   Beg

Work 1 row in pattern.

Working both sides at once with separate balls of yarn, work fully fashioned neck decreases (see Notes) at each neck edge every other row 6 times, then every 4 rows 6 times—17 stitches remain.

Work both sides even until the piece measures approximately 28 (28½, 28½, 29, 29, 29½)"/[71 (72, 72, 74, 74, 75)cm] from the beginning, ending after a wrong-side row.

SHAPE SHOULDERS
Work same as for the Back.

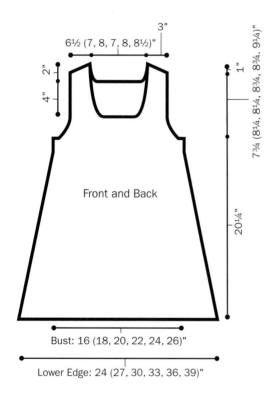

6½ (7, 8, 7, 8, 8½)"

3"

2"

4"

1"

7¾ (8¼, 8¼, 8¾, 8¾, 9¼)"

20¼"

Front and Back

Bust: 16 (18, 20, 22, 24, 26)"

Lower Edge: 24 (27, 30, 33, 36, 39)"

Finishing

Darn in all remaining yarn tails (page 156).

Block all pieces to the finished measurements (page 156).

Sew the shoulder seams.

ATTACHED I-CORD NECKBAND
Using the e-wrap method (page 150), cast 3 stitches onto a double-pointed needle, then pick up and knit 1 stitch at the center back neck of the garment. *Do not turn*. Slide the 4 stitches to the right-hand tip of the double-pointed needle, k2, ssk, pick up and knit 1 stitch from the neckline of the garment; repeat from the * around the neck opening.

Bind off.

Sew the ends of the I-Cord together.

Sew the side seams.

ATTACHED I-CORD ARMBAND
Using the e-wrap method (page 150), cast 3 stitches onto a double-pointed needle, then pick up and knit 1 stitch at the center underarm of the garment.

Continue working Attached I-Cord as for the neckband around the armhole.

Repeat for the other armhole.

General Knitting Techniques

Attaching New Yarn

Whenever possible, try to attach a new ball of yarn at the beginning of a row.

To start a new color of yarn at the beginning of a knit row: Drop the old yarn, insert your right-hand needle into the first stitch of the row as if you are about to knit, grab the new yarn, and use it to knit the first stitch (illustration 18). Always begin and end every yarn with at least a 6"/[15cm] tail. Otherwise you won't have enough length to weave it in sufficiently.

To start a new yarn at the beginning of a purl row: Drop the old yarn, insert your right-hand needle into that first stitch of the row as if you're about to purl rather than knit, and purl it.

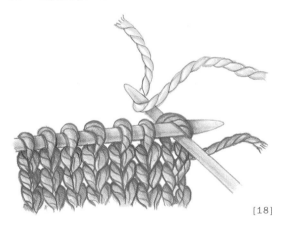

[18]

Bobbles

Bobbles introduce wonderful surface texture (not to mention, playful whimsy) to fabrics. While some knitters find them time-consuming to knit, they are not difficult to do. To make a bobble, work several stitches into a single stitch, increasing the number of stitches in that area from one stitch to three, five, or more. Work several rows on these new stitches, turning the work after each successive row. Finally, decrease the stitches back to the original single stitch.

There are several ways to knit a bobble, but here's my favorite. It's used in Angie (page 143): Knit into the (front, back, front) of a single stitch, turn; work into these same three stitches, p1, (p1, yarn over, p1) *all into the next stitch,* then p1, turn; knit the 5 stitches, turn; decrease from five stitches down to three stitches as follows: P2tog, p1, p2tog, turn. Finally, decrease from 3 stitches down to one stitch as follows: Slip 2 stitches at once knitwise, knit the next stitch, then pass the 2 slipped stitches from the right-hand needle over the last knit stitch as if you're binding them off.

Cable Cast-On

Here's my favorite cast-on technique: It's beautiful, easy, and quick to do. Plus, it's perfect when the first row worked is a right-side row.

Start by making a slip knot on your knitting needle, then insert the tip of the right-hand needle knitwise into the loop that's sitting on the left-hand needle and knit up a stitch (illustration 19) *but don't remove the original stitch from the left-hand needle;* instead, transfer the new stitch from the right-hand needle back to the left-hand one. One new stitch has been cast on.

[19]

For each successive stitch to be cast on, insert the tip of the right-hand needle *between* the first 2 stitches on the left-hand needle to knit up a stitch (illustration 20).

[20]

As before, do not remove the old stitch, rather slip the new one back onto the left-hand needle; repeat until you have cast on the required number of stitches.

Cables

Cables are created when stitches exchange places with other stitches within a knit row. One set of stitches is placed on a cable needle to keep them out of the way while another set of stitches is worked. Depending on whether those stitches are held to the front or to the back of the work, whether the cable uses two, three, or even seventeen stitches, and whether the stitches are ultimately knit or purled or any combination of the two, they create beautiful patterns. For a two-over-two right crossed stockinette cable, for example, slip 2 stitches onto a cable needle and *hold them in back of the work;* knit 2 stitches from the left-hand needle, then knit the 2 stitches from cable needle. For a two-over-two left crossed stockinette cable, slip 2 stitches onto a cable needle and *hold them in front of the work;* knit 2 stitches from the left-hand needle, then knit the 2 stitches from the cable needle.

E-Wrap Cast-On

Here's a quick cast-on method that is easy to do. It is not as stable as many other techniques.

To do: Wrap the yarn from front to back around your left thumb, then insert the right-hand needle from front to back to catch the strand (illustration 21).

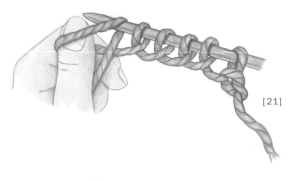

[21]

Fasten Off

To finish a piece of fabric securely once the knitting is completed, cut the yarn, leaving a tail at least 6"/ [15cm] long, and fasten off by drawing the loose tail through the remaining stitch on the knitting needle. Later, this yarn tail can be used for seaming or else must be woven in (page 156).

Knit a Stitch Through Its Back Loop (abbreviated k1-tbl)

This technique twists a stitch. It is often used to make stitches appear embossed on top of fabric.

To work this technique, just insert your right-hand needle into the indicated stitch from right to left and from front to back, and wrap the working yarn around the needle the regular way to knit the stitch (illustration 22).

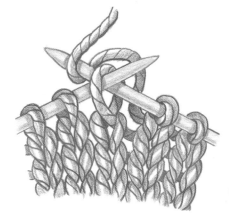

[22]

Knit in the Row Below

This technique is used to create novelty stitch patterns, such as the Fisherman's Rib in Candace's Shell (page 81).

To do: Simply insert the top of the right-hand needle into the stitch that's directly below the first stitch on the left-hand needle (illustration 23), and knit it. Slip off the left-hand needle.

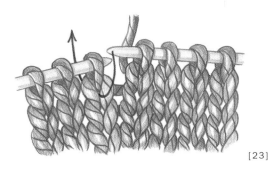

[23]

Knitwise

Instructions will sometimes tell you to insert your knitting needle into a stitch knitwise. To do this, simply insert the tip of your right-hand needle into the indicated stitch as if you were about to knit that stitch—in other words, from left to right and *from front to back* (illustration 24).

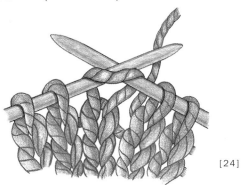

[24]

If you're told to slip a stitch knitwise, insert the tip of your right-hand needle into the indicated stitch as if you're about to knit it and slide that stitch off of the left-hand needle and onto the right-hand one, allowing the stitch to sit on the right-hand needle with its left "leg" in the front. Usually, stitches are slipped knitwise during a decrease.

Provisional Cast-On

Using smooth waste yarn in a highly contrasting color to your working yarn, crochet a loose chain that is 4 or 5 chains longer than the number of stitches you plan to cast on.

Cut the yarn and pull the end through the last chain made to secure it. Tie a loose knot on this tail to mark it as the one you'll use to later unravel the chain.

Turn the crocheted chain over and use a knitting needle to pick up and knit 1 stitch through the back loop of each crocheted chain (illustration 25) until you have cast on the appropriate number of stitches for your knit piece.

To expose the live stitches later on, undo the last chain (the one nearest the knotted tail), gently unzip the chain (illustration 26), and transfer the stitches onto a knitting needle. Since you'll be knitting on the opposite side of the crocheted chain, to get the correct stitch count, you may need to create an extra stitch at one edge.

[25]

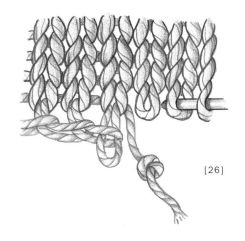

[26]

Purl a Stitch Through Its Back Loop (abbreviated P1-tbl)

Like knitting a stitch through the back loop, this technique twists a stitch.

To work this technique, just insert your right-hand needle into the indicated stitch from left to right and from back to front, and wrap the working yarn around the needle the regular way to purl the stitch (illustration 27).

[27]

Purlwise

When instructed to insert your knitting needle into a stitch purlwise, simply insert the tip of your right-hand needle into the indicated stitch as if you were about to purl that stitch—in other words, from right to left and *from back to front* (illustration 28).

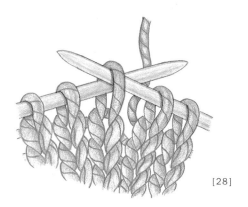

[28]

The convention in knitting is to always slip stitches purlwise unless told otherwise. When told to slip a stitch purlwise, insert the tip of your right-hand needle into the indicated stitch as if you're about to purl it and slide that stitch off of the left-hand needle and onto the right-hand one, allowing the stitch to sit on the right-hand needle with its right "leg" in the front.

Slip 2 Knit 1, Pass the 2 Slipped Stitches Over (abbreviated s2kp2)

Here's a central double decrease that takes 3 stitches down to 1 stitch.

To do it, slip 2 stitches at once knitwise (illustration 29), knit the next stitch (illustration 30), then pass the 2 slipped stitches over the stitch you just knit (illustration 31).

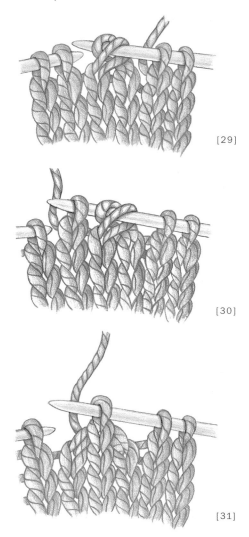

[29]

[30]

[31]

Steeks

Used primarily in stranded color knitting, steeks are extra stitches that are cast on and knit so the fabric can be worked completely in the round, making the colorwork easier to do; once the knitting is completed, the steek stitches are cut.

For the steek, a bridge of stitches is cast on using the e-wrap cast-on technique (illustration 21 on page 150) using alternating colors of yarn.

Usually, the steek stitches are knit in a simple color pattern, either in the same one-by-one vertical stripe pattern already set up in the cast-on or else in a simple alternating check pattern. Usually, a marker is placed on either side of the steek stitches to set them off from the main knitting.

After the knitting has been completed, unless the fabric has been worked in extremely sticky yarn such as Shetland wool, the steek edges are usually reinforced prior to cutting.

I recommend using single crochet stitches to secure things before cutting. Use a crochet hook at least 1–2 sizes smaller than your main knitting needle. And choose a highly contrasting yarn that's thinner than your main knitting yarn.

Single crochet stitches are worked to join the right-hand leg of one stitch to the left-hand leg of the adjacent stitch on either side of the cutting line. For example, let's look at a five-stitch steek and number the legs of each stitch (illustration 32).

Make a slip knot. Then turn your piece of knitting sideways and use a single crochet stitch to join Legs 4 and 5 for one column of stitches and then Legs 6 and 7 for

the second side. *This is one leg of the center stitch and one leg of the adjacent stitch.*

Begin securing the steek by inserting your crochet hook from front to back to front through the two legs (illustration 33).

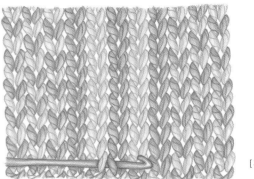

[33]

Place the reinforcement yarn onto the hook, yarn over the hook, and draw the yarn through the two legs (illustration 34).

[34]

1 2 3 4 5 6 7 8 9 10

[32]

Wrap the yarn over the hook, and draw it through the loop on the hook to complete a slip stitch. This maneuver attaches the crocheted chain to the knit fabric.

Insert the crochet hook into the next pair of legs, wrap the yarn over the hook and pull up a loop (you'll have two loops on the hook; illustration 35), then yarn over again and draw it through both loops to make a single crochet stitch.

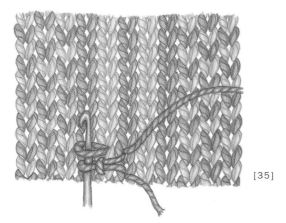

[35]

Repeat this last step to the top of the steek (illustration 36).

[36]

For the other side of the steek, turn your work in the other direction and, beginning at the bind-off row, work downward to join Legs 6 and 7. You will be joining the other leg of the center stitch with one leg of the adjacent stitch.

Once both legs of the center stitch are crocheted, the stitch will be pulled in two directions, leaving horizontal ladders right down the center between the legs—you can see this in the middle of the center stitch in illustration 37. This is where the steek will eventually be cut.

[37]

Once the steek has been secured, use the sharpest scissors you can find—in bright light, if possible—to cut the center of the steek. Be careful not to cut your crocheted reinforcing stitches!

Stranded Technique

In this color knitting technique, two colors are worked across each row, and when a color is not in use, it is carried loosely across the wrong side of the fabric, creating horizontal floats. Knitters can choose between 3 possible methods for holding the yarn:

Holding One Color in Each Hand

Here's the most efficient way to work stranded knitting: Hold one yarn in each hand, wrapping them around your fingers to control the tension the way you normally do (illustration 38). To work a stitch with the color from the right-hand yarn, insert the needle into the next stitch knitwise or purlwise according to your pattern, wrap the right-hand yarn around the needle to make either a knit or purl stitch; to make a stitch with the color of the yarn you're holding in your left hand, insert the needle into the next stitch knitwise or purlwise depending on your pattern, and wrap the left-hand yarn around the needle to complete the stitch.

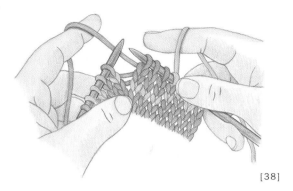

[38]

Holding Both Colors in the Right Hand

If you're normally an American-style "thrower," you can put both yarns in your right hand and use the appropriate color to knit or purl each stitch. Knitters have two possible methods to choose from.

METHOD 1: Loop both yarns around the right index finger (illustration 39). Use the bend of the top joint of your finger to keep the two yarns apart.

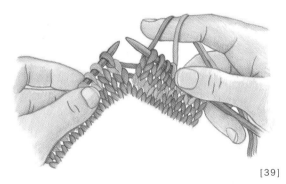

[39]

METHOD 2: Hold one color yarn over the index finger and the other color yarn over the middle finger (illustration 40).

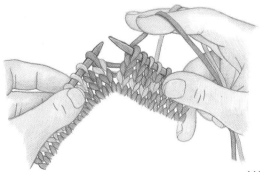

[40]

Holding Both Colors in the Left Hand

If you typically knit Continental-style, you can work with both yarns in your left hand. Again, knitters have two possible methods to choose from. With either method, the right-hand needle can easily "pick" the yarn called for in the color pattern.

METHOD 1: Place both color yarns over the left index finger (illustration 41). Use the bend of the top joint of your finger to keep the two yarns apart.

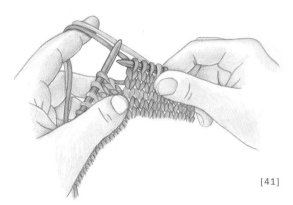

[41]

METHOD 2: Put one color yarn over the left index finger and the other color yarn over the middle finger (illustration 42).

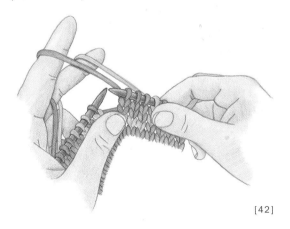

[42]

Finishing Techniques

Blocking

Prior to seaming your knit pieces, take the time to block them into shape. You'll be surprised at how this simple process can improve the appearance of your projects and can tame even the most unruly stitches! To do it, follow the laundering instructions on the yarn label for the most delicate yarn in your project, then use rustless pins to shape the damp fabric to your desired measurements and allow it to dry. Or gently steam the pieces into shape by placing a damp cloth over them and then carefully wafting a hot steam iron just above the fabric. Don't actually touch the iron to the fabric or you'll risk flattening it.

Hiding Yarn Tails

Use a pointed-end yarn needle to make short running stitches on the wrong side of your fabric in a diagonal line for about one inch or so, piercing the yarn strands that comprise the stitches of your fabric. Then, work back again to where you began, working alongside your previous running stitches. Finally, to secure the tail, work a stitch or two and actually pierce the running stitches you just created. Be sure to work each tail individually, in opposite diagonal directions, and you will secure your yarn ends while keeping the public side of your fabric neat and beautiful.

Mattress Stitch Seams

Here's the neatest seam imaginable for stockinette stitch and most knit fabrics. Nearly invisible, it can be worked vertically or horizontally.

For a Vertical Seam

Lay your pieces flat, with the right sides of the fabric facing you, matching patterns and stripes, if applicable.

Thread a blunt-end yarn needle with your sewing yarn, then bring the needle up *from back to front* through the left-hand piece of fabric, going in one stitch from the edge, leaving a 6"/[15cm] tail.

Bring the yarn up and through the corresponding spot on the right-hand piece to secure the lower edges.

Insert the needle *from front to back* into the same spot on the left-hand piece where the needle emerged last time and bring it up through the corresponding place of the next row of knitting.

Insert the needle *from front to back* into the same spot on the right-hand piece where the needle emerged last time and bring it up through the corresponding place of the next row of knitting.

Repeat the last two steps until you've sewn approximately 2"/[5cm], then pull firmly on the sewing yarn to bring the pieces of the fabric together, allowing the two stitches on the edges of each piece to roll to the wrong side.

Continue this way until your seam is complete (illustration 43).

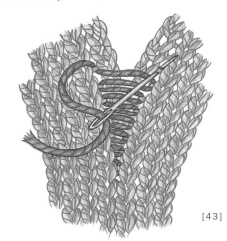

[43]

For a Horizontal Seam

Lay your pieces flat with the right sides of the fabric facing you and with the bound-off edges of the pieces together. Bring the needle up through the center of a stitch just below the bound-off edge on the lower piece of fabric, then insert it *from front to back* and from right to left around both legs of the corresponding stitch on the other piece of fabric. Bring the needle tip back down through the center of the same stitch where it first emerged.

Continue this way until your seam is complete (illustration 44).

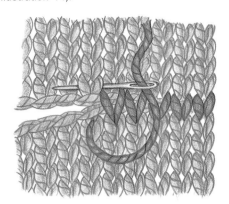

[44]

Sewing in a Zipper

Don't be afraid to add a zipper to a project! It's easy to do—and fun and convenient to wear. With the zipper closed and the right side of the garment pieces facing you, pin the zipper into place, keeping in mind that with hairier fabrics it might be best to allow more of the teeth to show, so the fibers don't get caught in the zipper's operation. Use contrasting sewing thread to baste the zipper into place (illustration 45).

Remove the pins and, with matching sewing thread, whipstitch the tape to the wrong side (illustration 46). Finally, with the right side of the garment facing you, use backstitch to sew down the zipper tape neatly (illustration 47). Fold any excess zipper tape to the wrong side and tack it down.

Whipstitch

This type of seam is used to secure a knit-in hem.

To do: Fold the facing of the hem to the wrong side of the fabric. Insert the tip of a blunt-tipped yarn needle into a stitch on the wrong side of the main fabric and then into the cast-on edge of the hem, drawing the yarn through (illustration 48).

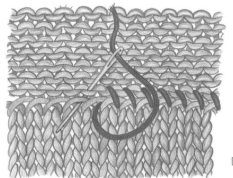

[48]

[45]

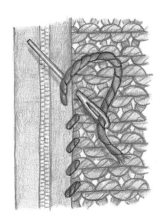

[46]

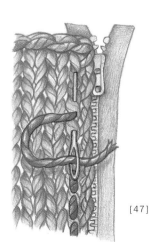

[47]

Sweater Assembly

Sweater pieces fit together like a jigsaw puzzle, with the type of armhole determining how the Front, Back, and Sleeves interlock. Refer to the illustrations below when assembling sweaters.

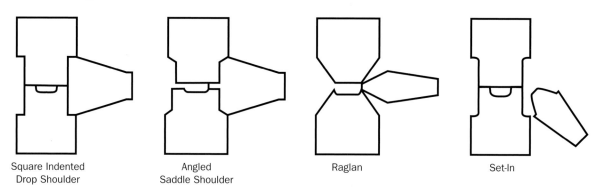

Square Indented
Drop Shoulder

Angled
Saddle Shoulder

Raglan

Set-In

Yarn Choice and Substitution

Each project in this book was designed for a specific yarn. Different yarns possess their own characteristics, which will affect the way they appear and behave when knit. To duplicate the projects exactly as photographed, I suggest that you use the designated yarns. Even so, you'll find that the nature of any handmade garment assures subtle differences and variances.

However, if you would like to make a yarn substitution, be sure to choose one of similar weight to the one called for in the pattern. Yarn sizes and weights are usually located on the label, but for an accurate test, knit a swatch of stockinette stitch pattern using the recommended needle size, making it at least 4"/[10cm] square.

Count the number of stitches in this 4"/[10cm] swatch and refer to the table below to determine the yarn's weight.

Yarn Size and Weight		Description	Stitches per 4"/[10cm] in Stockinette Stitch
1	Super Fine	Fingering weight	27 or more
2	Fine	Sport weight	23–26 sts
3	Light	DK weight	21–24 sts
4	Medium	Worsted weight	16–20 sts
5	Bulky	Bulky weight	12–15 sts
6	Super Bulky	Super Bulky weight	11 or fewer

Resources

Materials

I always recommend purchasing supplies at your local yarn shop. If there isn't one in your area, contact the appropriate wholesaler below for more information.

Brown Sheep Company
100662 County Road 16
Mitchell, NE 69357
(308) 635-2198
www.brownsheep.com

Cascade Yarns
1224 Andover Park E
Tukwila, WA 98188
(206) 574-0440
www.cascadeyarns.com

Classic Elite Yarns
122 Western Avenue
Lowell, MA 01851
(978) 453-2837
www.classiceliteyarns.com

GGH Yarns
(See Muench Yarns)

Jade Sapphire
148 Germonds Rd.
West Nyack, NY 10995
(845) 623-9036
www.jadesapphire.com

Jamieson's
(See Simply Shetland)

JCA, Inc.
35 Scales Lane
Townsend, MA 01469
(978) 597-8794
www.jcacrafts.com

JHB International, Inc.
1955 South Quince Street
Denver, CO 80231
(303) 751-8100
www.buttons.com

Knit One Crochet Too
91 Tandberg Trail, Unit 6
Windham, ME 04062
(207) 892-9625
www.knitonecrochettoo.com

Lion Brand Yarn
135 Kero Road
Carlstadt, NJ 07072
(800) 258-9276
www.lionbrand.com

Louet North America
3425 Hands Road
Prescott, ON, Canada K0E 1T0
(613) 925-4502
www.louet.com

Muench Yarns
1323 Scott Street
Petaluma, CA 94954
(707) 763-9377
www.muenchyarns.com

Plymouth Yarn Company
500 Lafayette Street
PO Box 28
Bristol, PA 19007
(215) 788-0459
www.plymouthyarn.com

Reynolds Yarn
(See JCA, Inc.)

Rowan Yarn
(See Westminster Fibers)

Simply Shetland
18435 Olympic Avenue South
Seattle, WA 98188
(877) 743-8526
http://simplyshetland.net/

Skacel Collection
PO Box 88110
Seattle, WA 98138
(425) 291-9600
www.skacelknitting.com

Trendsetter Yarns
16745 Saticoy St., Suite 101
Van Nuys, CA 91406
(818) 780-5497
www.trendsetteryarns.com

Westminster Fibers
165 Ledge St.
Nashua, NH 03060
(603) 886-5041
www.westminsterfibers.com

Yarn Sisters
475 Scrub Oak Circle
Monument, CO 80132
(719) 481-2900
www.theyarnsisters.com

Zealana Yarns
(See Yarn Sisters)

The Knitting Community

To meet other knitters and to learn more about the craft, contact the following. I currently sit on the Advisory Board and can attest to the educational value—and the pure, knitterly fun—of this great group.

The Knitting Guild Association
1100-H Brandywine Boulevard
Zanesville, OH 43701-7303
(740) 452-4541
E-mail: TKGA@TKGA.com
www.tkga.com

To meet other knitters online, visit:

www.ravelry.com

Index

Note: Page numbers in *italics* indicate patterns.